Coaching Mi... ~occei

A Tried and Tested Program of Essential Skills and Drills for 5 to 10 year olds.

Written By
Richard Seedhouse

Published By

Coaching Mini-Soccer
**A Tried and Tested Program of Essential
Skills and Drills for 5 to 10 year olds.**

First Published October 2010 by SoccerTutor.com
2 Churchview Buildings, The Green, Chingford, London, E4 7EL, UK
UK: 0208 1234 007 | **US:** (305) 767 4443 | **ROTW:** +44 208 1234 007

ISBN 978-0-9566752-0-0

Author
Richard Seedhouse © 2010

Edited by
Richard Seedhouse and SoccerTutor.com

Cover Design by
Alex Macrides, Think Out Of The Box Ltd.
email: info@thinkootb.com Tel: +44 (0) 208 144 3550

Diagrams
Diagram design by Richard Seedhouse. All the diagrams in this book have been created using SoccerTutor.com Tactics Manager Software available from **www.SoccerTutor.com**

Note: While every effort has been made to ensure the technical accuracy of the content of this book, neither the author nor publishers can accept any responsibility for any injury or loss sustained as a result of the use of this material.

Contents

Extra Drills

Preparation Drills for our Youngest Players and New Teams

v

Acknowledgements

This book would not exist without the continual support of www. SoccerTutor.com. It is they who identified the need for a successful coaching program to be made available for people involved in the development of younger players.

This program has been developed over a number of years and through practical sessions and discussions with many great friends and coaches. Thanks therefore need to go to everyone who has helped but specifically a few coaches who have been most supportive to me personally. Thanks therefore need to go to Barry Morris, Terry Harvey, Stuart Wilson, Paul Reynolds, Steve Ellis, Ian Weaving, Richard Steeples and Tom Stack for their influence and help over the years. Special thanks also to everyone at Coundon Court FC and Birmingham County FA especially Heidi Lockyer.

Can I also thank Thomas Poole and his family for their kind permission to use the wonderful photograph on the front cover.

I would also like to take this opportunity to thank my wife, Kirsten for putting up with me and all things Football. Thanks and I love you.

Special thanks and appreciation has to go to Chris Morris, without whom there would be no Coundon Court FC, no journey into coaching and coach education, no coaching program and therefore no books.

"For Luke"

Introduction

This book is the conclusion to years of coach education and practical experience in coaching young players. "Tried and Tested", this coaching program has produced academy standard players year on year. "Results", In the last three years eight children have been signed by professional clubs for their academies at U9. Our grassroot teams (U8 and U9) are regularly asked to attend and play against other regional clubs and academy teams at Professional club trials.

This book contains the 12 sessions Coundon Court FC (A National Award Winning Football Association Charter Standard Community Club) have used year on year to develop these players. The program in its simplest form (for younger players) is the community soccer coaching program it operates each Saturday morning. The one hour sessions are used for coaching children at ages 5 and 6. The better players at 6 and 7 experience the progressions and technical games to prepare them for mini-soccer, the 7 v 7 format. The small sided games and further progressions are added as the players ability develops and teams are formed from the community sessions year on year.

The more clubs that effectively coach technique, and skills while utilising both small sided games and technical games can only be good for the progression and development of our players. It is to this end that we offer this book.

Please note this program needs coaches who will challenge the players and inject fun into the sessions. The coach needs to understand how, what and why they coach. For further reading on coach education and development new coaches should combine this program with the best selling soccer coaching book "Coaching The Coach" Many of the drills appear in both books but in "Coaching The Coach" we concentrate on developing the coach to develop the players. It is coach education and development combined with a proven player development program that is needed to drive the game forward.

Session Format

Basic Overview

Each coaching session lasts for 1 hour and is split into three distinct sections.

1.   The Warm Up.

This always takes place within a 20x20 yard coned square. This is so all the players understand where to go when they get to the session. It also keeps them in a safe area both while we wait to begin and during the session. When players arrive and register they receive a ball each and play within the square whilst the coach waits for everyone to arrive and for the session to start.

Created Using www.SoccerTutor.com Tactics Manager Software

Warm Up - Ball Work

The Warm up continues each week with a different technical skill, turn or move being coached within the square.

Remember

At the end of each warm up and ball work section make sure you give the players a couple of minutes to experiment. Give two rules - 1) They are not allowed outside the square 2) The ball has to stay on the floor.

This time is now used for the players to dribble around the square and practice the technical skills, turns and moves coached each week.

2.   The Drill

Each week a different specific drill is used to coach the fundamental skills required in football. Heading, Shooting, Dribbling, Passing, Defending and Goalkeeping are all coached over the twelve weeks. Extra drills are included at the back of the book, two relate to each session plan.

A diagram shows each drill and is accompanied by an explanation of the Organization and a description of the drill.

Key

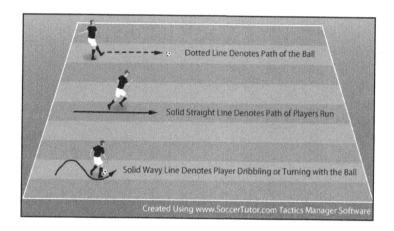

Dotted Line Denotes Path of the Ball

Solid Straight Line Denotes Path of Players Run

Solid Wavy Line Denotes Player Dribbling or Turning with the Ball

Created Using www.SoccerTutor.com Tactics Manager Software

3.   The End Game

The session always finishes with the end game. These will be either structured tactical 7-a-side games promoting formations and team shape or small sided games to promote technique and skills.

With the younger players you may want to go straight into a standard game but as you begin to prepare your players for mini soccer you should use the technical games and preparation drills at the back of the book

When your players are older and understand the formations better you will be able to use the small sided games. These will enhance the technical ability and skills of your players whilst developing their problem solving within a game situation.

Session 1 - Quick Shooting

Session Objective	Shooting - Coach to Improve Quick Shooting
Duration	1 Hour
Equipment	First Aid Kit, Mobile Phone, Ball for each Player, 3x sets of Bibs, Disc Marker Cones, 4 x Traffic Cones, 4 x Target Goals, Ball Pump, Whistle, Register.

Warm Up - Ball Work

Created Using www.SoccerTutor.com Tactics Manager Software

Organization

Always begin with the same warm up within the 20x20 yard coned square. The warm up should consist of Jogging, forward, backward and sideways movement, knees up and bum kicks, hoping, skipping and jumping.

Progression - Ball Work - One Foot Dribbling

The players have one ball each and dribble about within the square using both feet, inside, outside, sole and laces. In this session we want to promote comfort on the ball with either foot so challenge your players to only use one foot. After a couple of minutes challenge them to only use the other foot.

Give the players a couple of minutes to dribble about practising their skills.

Fun

Can they go faster? Can they switch from using only one foot to the other as the coach shouts change?

Drill - Quick Shooting

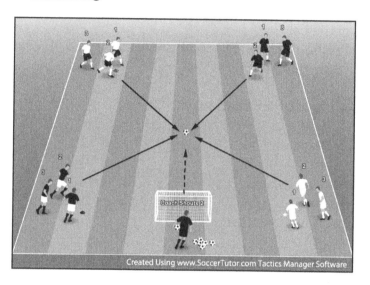

Created Using www.SoccerTutor.com Tactics Manager Software

Organization

A 20 x 20 yard square is marked out with four different colour cones at each corner. The players are split into four teams and each team lines up in a corner. Each player in the team is given a number. Try and match the numbered players in all the teams in terms of size and ability.

Description

The drill begins with the coach standing behind the goal shouting a number (in this case 2) and throwing a ball over the goal. The player from each team who has that number runs out to try and score a goal. Once a shot is taken and a goal scored or the ball goes out of play the players return to their cones / corners and the drill is repeated with the coach shouting another number.

Coaching Points to Improve Shooting in this drill.

1. Approach – Sprint to the ball directly to get there as quickly as possible. Shoot whenever and as soon as the possibility arises.
2. Body Shape - The standing foot should be planted next to the ball with the toes pointing towards the goal whilst allowing space for the kicking foot to swing through. The head should be steady, knee over the ball and arms out for balance.
3. Contact – The shot should be taken with the foot nearest to the ball so there is no delay. The laces of the boot should contact through the centre of the ball.
4. Follow through - A short but sharp and strong follow through to keep the ball down and accurate.

Progressions and Drill Variations

For Younger Players.

1. Make the pitch smaller.
2. No goalkeeper.
3. Bigger goals to make scoring easier.

For Older or Better Players.

Created Using www.SoccerTutor.com Tactics Manager Software

1. Smaller target goals.
2. Add a goalkeeper.
3. Make the pitch bigger.
4. Move teams around so they all get to start at each corner cone.
5. The coach shouts more than one number.
6. Add a time limit in which to score or shoot.

Fun

Use the different coloured cone in each corner as the team name, i.e. red team, blue team, white team and encourage players to cheer on their own team by name, "come on the reds" etc. Keep score of all the goals scored by the teams to see which team wins.

End Game - Quick Shooting

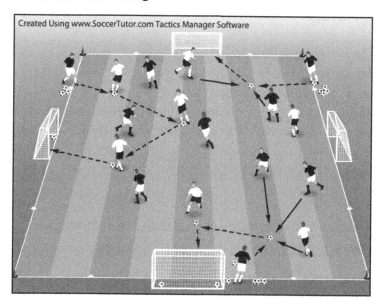

Created Using www.SoccerTutor.com Tactics Manager Software

Organization

A 20 x 20 yard square marked with cones. Four goals are set up midway along each side. All the players are split into two teams. The coach and assistants stand around the side of the square with plenty of balls each.

Description

The coach starts the game by rolling a ball into the square. The assistants also add balls, try to keep 3 or 4 balls in play all the time. The teams compete to win a ball and score a goal in any of the goals around the square.

Progressions and Drill Variations

For Younger Players

1. Use only 1 or 2 balls and stop the game frequently.
2. Try three or four teams of players.
3. Use bigger goals.

For Older Players

1. Use a larger square 30 x 30.
2. Smaller target goals.
3. Two small target goals on each side.
4. Split the players into four teams of four players, each team having a goalkeeper. The teams can only score in the three opposing teams goals.

Fun

Keep the scores and add competition with the first team to score five goals winning.

Adding extra balls will add to the chaos, speed and fun of scoring more goals more often. Add extra balls at anytime. Always remove the goalkeeper if you add more balls as more than one shot could be hit toward them.

Small Sided Game

Created Using www.SoccerTutor.com Tactics Manager Software

Organization

To use this drill as a small sided game simply reduce the teams to four a side and only have one ball in play at any one time.

Question and Coach the Players?

1. Why do you need to get to the ball as quickly as possible? To win possession.
2. When should you shoot? As soon as you get the chance.
3. Which foot should you shoot with? The foot that is closest to the ball or gets to the ball without breaking your stride.
4. What about your positioning? Can you get into positions to receive the ball in space and near an opponents goal.
5. Which goal should you shoot at? The nearest goal or the one you are facing and have the first chance to shoot at.
6. Were you ready, did you see the ball? When two or more balls are in play the players should be ever alert, where is the nearest ball and goal?

End the session by removing two of the goals and leaving a standard pitch. The players can now finish the session playing the game they love.

Session 2 - Short Passing

Session Objective   Passing - Coach to Improve Short Passing

Duration   1 Hour

Equipment   First Aid Kit, Mobile Phone, Ball for each Player, 2 x sets of Bibs, Disc Marker Cones, 4 x Traffic Cones, 2 x Goals, Ball Pump, Whistle, Register.

Warm Up - Ball Work

Organization

Always begin with the same warm up within the 20x20 yard coned square. The warm up should consist of Jogging, forward, backward and sideways movement, knees up and bum kicks, hoping, skipping and jumping.

Progression - Ball Work - "Scissors" Move

The players have one ball each and dribble about within the square using both feet, inside, outside, sole and laces. In this session we want to coach the "Scissors" move.

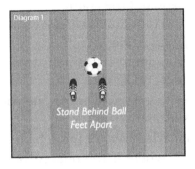

Diagram 1

Stand Behind Ball
Feet Apart

Diagram 2

Bring Feet Together

Sweep the Foot Clockwise Around the Front of the Ball Pretending to Take the Ball Away to the Right

Quickly Change Direction Taking the Ball Away to the Left with the Outside Of the Other Foot

To start the move both feet are placed behind the ball. The left foot should be placed wide to the left to enable the right foot to sweep low around the ball clockwise from a 5 O'clock position to a 2 O'clock position. The ball is then taken away with the outside of the other foot, in this case the left foot. Promote practising the skill using both feet.

Coaching Younger Players

When coaching the very young players, or players who struggle to go clockwise around the ball, break the move down into four steps.

1. Stand behind the ball feet apart (diagram 1)
2. Bring the right foot behind the ball and across next to the left foot. This should stop them going around the ball anti-clockwise first and getting their legs tangled (diagram 2)
3. Then sweep the right foot forward around the front of the ball and back to where it was (diagram 3)
4. Kick the ball with the other foot, once they get used to kicking with the other foot move onto the outside of the other foot (diagram 4)

Coaching Older Players

1. The older players should try and attempt the double "Scissors". This is when both feet go around the ball prior to taking it away.
2. Encourage the player to exaggerate the movement or dummy to go right. Can they drop their shoulder?

Give the players a couple of minutes to dribble about practising their skills.

Drill - Passing Gates

Created Using www.SoccerTutor.com Tactics Manager Software

Organization

A 20 x 20 yard square is marked out with four traffic cones and filled with a series of gates made up of two marker cones. The players are split into pairs and each pair is given a ball. The players stand opposite each other and either side of a gate. Make sure you have more gates than pairs of players.

Description

The players simply pass the ball to each other through the gates. The players should try and trap the ball with the instep and pass the ball with the instep.

Coaching Points to Improve Passing in this drill.

Demonstrate and explain these coaching points to our players.

1. Approach – Slightly from the side to give enough room to make a comfortable pass. If the player moves straight onto the ball then there is a possibility to toe poke the ball.
2. Body Shape - The standing foot should be planted next to the ball with the toes pointing in the direction of the intended pass with an open body to allow room for the side foot pass. The head should be steady and arms out for balance.

3. Contact – The instep or inside of the foot (the largest area) of the boot should contact through the centre of the ball for a pass along the ground.
4. Follow through – This helps accuracy and power. The follow through should be in line with the intended pass to keep it accurate. The more follow through the more powerful the pass.

Progressions and Drill Variations

For Younger Players.

1. Make the gates bigger.
2. Increase the number of gates.

For Older or Better Players.

1. Smaller gates.
2. Add a time limit.
3. One touch passing.
4. Alternate the trap and pass, trap with left foot and pass with right and alternate for the next trap and pass.
5. Add movement by making the players dribble to another set of gates to make the next pass, moving on again before each pass.

Fun

How many passes can be made in a set time?
Did the pass go cleanly through the gates, don't let the ball touch the cones.

Top Tips

Pass with the instep of the foot; control, weight and accuracy of the pass.
Always be ready to receive a pass, on your toes.
Communicate with your partner, point and show where the next gate is.

End Game - Thirds Game

Created Using www.SoccerTutor.com Tactics Manager Software

Organization

A 50 x 30 yard pitch is marked out with four traffic cones in the corners and marker cones all around. You may need to change the size of the pitch to make it more suitable to the size and power of your players. Place marker cones across the pitch to split it into three thirds.

Description

In this tactical game use the thirds to show our players the positions on the field and promote passing. Each team is split into a typical mini soccer formation (in this case 2,3,1). The players cannot move from their designated third, defenders stay in the defensive third, midfielders in the central third and strikers in the attacking third. The only way a team can score is to pass the ball through the thirds to their striker. Remember to rotate players so they experience playing in all the positions.

Question and Coach the Players?

How can you help the player with the ball who wants to play a pass?

1. Get into space.
2. Can the player clearly see a path for the ball to get to them.
3. Call the name of the player with the ball to tell them you are in a position and want to receive the ball.

End the session by removing the thirds leaving a standard pitch. The players can now finish the session playing a normal game.

Session 3 - Possession

Session Objective	Passing - Coach to Improve Retaining Possession
Duration	1 Hour
Equipment	First Aid Kit, Mobile Phone, Ball for each Player, 2 x sets of Bibs, Disc Marker Cones, 4 x Traffic Cones, Goals, Ball, Pump, Whistle, Register.

Warm Up - Ball Work

Organization

Always begin with the same warm up within the 20x20 yard coned square. The warm up should consist of dynamic stretching. Jogging, forward, backward and sideways movement, knees up and bum kicks, hoping, skipping and jumping.

Progression - Ball Work - Retaining Possession

The players have one ball each and dribble about within the square using both feet, inside, outside, sole and laces. In this session we want to coach our players to keep possession of the ball.

Created Using www.SoccerTutor.com Tactics Manager Software

Description

Take two or three players out of the square and take the balls off them (shown above in blue) These players are now the defenders and on the coach's command they enter the square and try to kick out all of the other players balls.

Fun

The defenders can be given names like "Monsters" or "Killers".
The last two players remaining in the square in possession of their balls become the defenders for the next game.

<u>Drill - Shielding</u>

Created Using www.SoccerTutor.com Tactics Manager Software

Organization

A 20 x 20 yard square is marked out with four traffic cones and marker cones. The players are split into two teams and then a player from each team are paired together. Try and match the players by size and ability.

Description

All of the player's from one of the teams start with a ball and they dribble about within the square. The player paired with them from the other team tries to win the ball and gain possession. If the ball goes out of the square or if they win the ball then it is their turn to try and keep possession of the ball.

Coaching Points to Improve Shielding the Ball.

1. Observation - The player with the ball should know where the defender is at all times either by looking or feeling.
2. Body Shape - Can the player keep their body between the ball and the defender. Keep a long barrier when the defender is close.
3. Technique - Control the ball away from the defender. For example if the defender is to the right the player should use the outside of the left foot to manoeuvre the ball away to the left.

Progressions and Drill Variations

For Younger Players.

1. Make the area bigger.
2. Give a short time limit.

For Older or Better Players.

1. Make the area smaller.

Fun

As there is a player from each team in each pair we can stop the drill after a certain amount of time and add up how many players from each team have possession of the ball. We can then see which team has the most balls and therefore wins. Each drill should restart with all the players from one team having the ball and this team should be switched before each restart.

End Game - Don't Loose Possession

Organization

A 20 x 20 yard square marked with cones. The players are split into six attackers and two defenders. The two defenders should hold a visible bib in one of their hands.

Created Using www.SoccerTutor.com Tactics Manager Software

Description

The six attackers play keep ball with the two defenders trying to win possession of the ball. If a defender wins the ball they throw the bib they are holding on the floor and become an attacker. The attacker who lost possession of the ball picks up the bib and becomes a defender.

Fun

Throwing the bib on the floor for the next person has its own element of fun along with the competition of winning the ball back.

<u>Question and Coach the Players?</u>

Does the player with the ball need to pass it? No, they can retain possession by shielding the ball until a teammate becomes available.

This drill will need perseverance with younger players, so knowing your players and their ability to understand this drill is critical.

End the session by adding goals to make a standard pitch. The players can now finish the session by playing football.

Session 4 - Running With The Ball

Session Objective   Coach to Improve Running with the Ball

Duration   1 Hour

Equipment   First Aid Kit, Mobile Phone, Ball for each Player, 2 x sets of Bibs, Disc Marker Cones, 4 x Traffic Cones, 2x Goals, Ball Pump, Whistle, Register.

Warm Up - Ball Work

Organization

Always begin with the same warm up within the 20x20 yard coned square. The warm up should consist of dynamic stretching. Jogging, forward, backward and sideways movement, knees up and bum kicks, hoping, skipping and jumping.

Progression - Ball Work - "Drag Back" Turn

The players have one ball each and dribble about within the square using both feet, inside, outside, sole and laces. In this session we want to coach the "Drag Back" turn.

Dribble the Ball Forward Using both Feet

Stop the Ball by Putting the Sole of the Right Foot on the Top of the Ball

Diagram 3

Drag the Ball Backwards
Using the Sole of the Foot

Diagram 4

Now The Player can Turn
and Dribble the Ball Back in
the Direction they Came.

To start the turn the players dribble the ball forward before stopping the ball with the sole of the foot (in this case the right foot) The sole of the foot then drags the ball backwards behind the player who can then turn and take the ball away in the opposite direction. The players should practice the "Drag Back" turn using both their right and left feet.

Coaching Younger Players

When coaching the very young players for the first time break the move down into four steps and coach them in the logical order.

1. Dribble forward slowly (diagram 1)
2. Use the sole of the right foot to reach forward and stop the ball by placing it on the top of the ball (diagram 2).
3. Use the right foot to drag the ball backwards. Remember to make sure your players look behind them before doing this turn (diagram 3)
4. The player can now turn 180 degrees and dribble the ball away (diagram 4)

Coaching Older Players

1. The players should try the "Drag Back" with the left foot as well as the right, simply have the left foot stopping and dragging back the ball back instead of the right.
2. Encourage the player to exaggerate the movement or dummy to go forward prior to stopping the ball and moving back in the opposite direction.

Drill - Running with the Ball

Organization

Created Using www.SoccerTutor.com Tactics Manager Software

Use marker cones and traffic cones to set out a 20x30 yard rectangle. Use the two similar cones to mark the two corners diagonally opposite each other. The players are split with half of them standing at each of the diagonally opposite corners marked with the normal marker cones.

Description

The first player in each queue has a ball and on the coaches command runs with the ball directly at the traffic cone ahead. The players have to sprint straight at the cone ahead of them and not toward the line of players opposite. When they get within 5 yards of the traffic cone they pass the ball diagonally across to the first player in the other line. That player can then sprint forward with the ball and repeat the drill.

Coaching Points to Improve Running With The Ball.

1. Attitude - The player needs a positive attitude and a positive first touch. The younger players should let the ball come across their body before taking a positive touch forward with the instep of the back foot.
2. Head Up - The player should have their head up in between touches.
3. Contact - The laces of the nearest boot should contact through the centre of the ball. They should not break their stride pattern to always play the ball with their favoured foot.
4. End product – The final pass needs to be played in front of the next player.

Progressions and Drill Variations

For Younger Players.

1. Make the area smaller in length.

For Older or Better Players.

1. Make the area longer.
2. Allow the first player in each team to start with a ball so you always have two players running.
3. Can the players sprint straight at the ball being passed across to them taking a positive first touch with the nearest foot to the ball.

Fun

When we have two players sprinting simultaneously can they catch the other player up?

End Game - Running Wing Game

Organization

Created Using www.SoccerTutor.com Tactics Manager Software

A 60 x 40 yard pitch is marked out with four traffic cones in the corners and marker cones all around. You may need to change the size of the pitch to make it more suitable to the size and power of your players. Place marker cones along each side of the pitch to create channels, approximately 5 foot wide and also add a half way line.

Description

In this tactical game the sides line up with a goalkeeper, three defenders and two attackers. There are two neutral wide players, 1 in each of the channels. No other player can enter the channel. The only way the ball can get from the defenders to the attackers is via a neutral winger. The winger should receive the ball from a defender in one half of the pitch and run with the ball unopposed into the other half before crossing the ball into the attackers.

End Game Variations

If you do not have a goalkeeper then just use small target goals or use one target goal and a standard goal if you only have one goalkeeper. If you are short of a few players then reduce the 3v2 overload in each half to just a 2v1 overload.

Question and Coach the Players?

Where does the winger want the ball played and why?

1. The ball should be passed ahead of the winger so they can run onto the ball at speed and take it along the channel as fast as possible before crossing to the attackers.
2. Demonstrate and coach all the key points we have listed for running with the ball.
3. Swap the neutral players so everyone gets the chance to play as the winger and practice running with the ball.

End the session by removing the channels so the players can play normally.

Session 5 - Passing

Session Objective   Coach to Improve Passing and movement

Duration   1 Hour

Equipment   First Aid Kit, Mobile Phone, Ball for each Player, 2 x sets of Bibs, Disc Marker Cones, 2 x Target Goals, 4x Traffic Cones, Ball Pump, Whistle, Register.

Warm Up - Ball Work

Organization

Always begin with the same warm up within the 20x20 yard coned square. The warm up should consist of dynamic stretching. Jogging, forward, backward and sideways movement, knees up and bum kicks, hoping, skipping and jumping.

Progression - Ball Work - "Cruyff" Turn

The players have one ball each and dribble about within the square using both feet, inside, outside, sole and laces. In this session we want to coach the "Cruyff" turn.

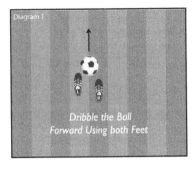

Diagram 1

Dribble the Ball Forward Using both Feet

Diagram 2

Swing the Right Foot Extravagantly As if Crossing or Passing the Ball a Long Way over to the Left.

Stop the Right Foot Directly Ahead of the Ball and Draw it Backwards Using the Inside of the Right Foot.

Now The Player can Turn and Dribble the Ball Back in the Direction they Came.

To start the turn the players dribble the ball forward before faking to cross or shoot. The player should swing their foot (in this case the right foot) and stop it just in front of the ball. The instep of the foot can then be used to knock the ball backwards behind the players standing foot. They can then turn and take the ball away in the opposite direction. The players should practice the "Cruyff" turn using both their right and left feet.

Coaching Younger Players

When coaching the very young players for the first time break each of the four steps down and explain them in the logical order.

1. Dribble forward slowly (diagram 1)
2. Exaggerate a cross but swing the foot ahead of the ball and stop the foot just in front of the ball (diagram 2).
3. Use the inside of the right foot through the centre of the ball knocking it behind the standing foot (diagram 3)
4. The player can now turn 180 degrees and dribble the ball away (diagram 4)

Coaching Older Players

1. The players should try the "Cruyff Turn" with the left foot as well as the right. Simply fake the cross / shot with the left foot, stop it ahead of the ball and drag it back.
2. Encourage the player to exaggerate the movement or dummy to cross or shoot in order to fool the defender before moving back in the opposite direction.

Drill - Passing by Numbers

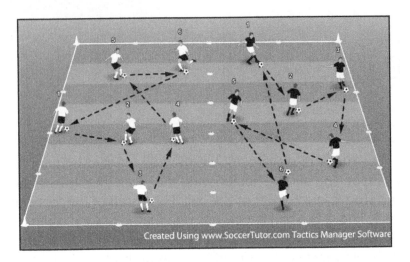

Organization

Set out a 20x20 yard square using marker cones with traffic cones in the corners and put in a half way line. Split the players into two teams and put each team in one side of the square.

Description

Number the players in each team. Only one ball is used for each team. Number 1 passes to number 2, who passes to number 3, who passes to 4 etc. The number 6 passes the ball back to the first player and the drill continues.

Coaching Points to Improve Passing in this drill.

1. Approach – Slightly from the side to give enough room to make a comfortable pass.
2. Body Shape - The standing foot should be planted next to the ball with the toes pointing in the direction of the intended pass with an open body. The head should be steady and arms out for balance.
3. Contact – The instep or inside of the foot (the largest area) of the boot should contact through the centre of the ball for a pass along the ground.
4. Follow through – The follow through should be in line with the

intended pass to keep it accurate. The more follow through the more powerful the pass.

Progressions and Drill Variations

For Younger Players.

1. Only have one team of 12 in the whole 20x20 area.

For Older or Better Players.

1. Give each team more than one ball.
2. Take out the half way line and make the players from both teams move about sharing the whole area whilst still playing in their individual teams.

Fun

How many balls can they cope with being passed around, which player does the second ball catch up with while they still have the first? Add a competition, which team passes the ball all the way round and back to player number 1 first.

End Game - Inside Out Soccer

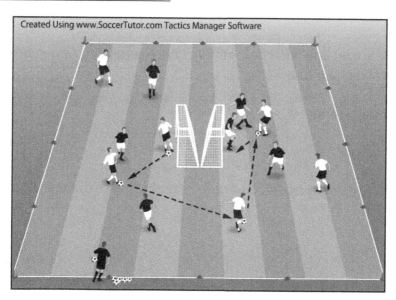

Created Using www.SoccerTutor.com Tactics Manager Software

Organization

A 20x20 yard square is set up with marker cones and traffic cones in the corners. Two goals are placed back to back in the centre of the area facing outward. All the players are split into two teams.

Description

The teams pass the ball around the goals (as shown) to score in the opponents goal. They cannot pass the ball over the goals.

Progressions and Drill Variations

For Younger Players

1. Use larger goals and no goalkeepers.

For Older Players

1. Use smaller target goals.
2. Add goalkeepers.
3. Mark a half way line and use dedicated defenders and attackers in the two halves.

Fun

Keep the scores and add competition. Give the teams a target, first team to score five goals wins.

Small Sided Game

Organization

To use this drill as a small sided game simply reduce the teams to four a side.

Created Using www.SoccerTutor.com Tactics Manager Software

Question and Coach the Players?

What can you coach?

1. The players on the team with the ball need to get into space and more importantly into a position where the player with the ball can pass to you.
2. Call the name of the player with the ball to tell them you want the ball and are in a position to receive it.
3. Watch the play and see if you can see an error from a player making a pass. Coach the technical points of the pass in a logical order.

End the session by extending the area and moving the goals to the ends. The players can now finish the session playing a standard game of soccer.

Session 6 - Dribbling

Session Objective   Coach to improve Dribbling and Wing play.

Duration   1 Hour

Equipment   First Aid Kit, Mobile Phone, Ball for each Player, 2 x sets of Bibs, Disc Marker Cones, 2 x Target Goals, 4 x Traffic Cones, Ball Pump, Whistle, Register.

Warm Up - Ball Work

Organization

Always begin with the same warm up within the 20x20 yard coned square. The warm up should consist of dynamic stretching. Jogging, forward, backward and sideways movement, knees up and bum kicks, hoping, skipping and jumping.

Progression - Ball Work - "Stop" Turn

The players have one ball each and dribble about within the square using both feet, inside, outside, sole and laces. In this session we want to coach the "Stop" turn.

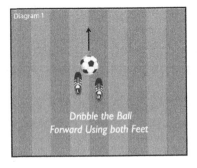

Dribble the Ball
Forward Using both Feet

Stop the Ball by Putting
the Sole of the Right Foot
on the Top of the Ball

Take the Right Foot off the Ball
Before Continuing the Jump over it
Land Side on (As if on a Surf Board).

Use the Outside of the Left Foot
to Play the Ball Backwards

To start the turn the players dribble the ball forward before stopping the ball with the sole of the foot (in this case the right foot) and then jumping over the ball. The outside of the back foot (in this case the Left foot) nearest the ball then plays the ball backwards. The players should practice the "Stop" turn using both their right and left feet.

Coaching Younger Players

When coaching the very young players for the first time demonstrate each of the four steps in the logical order.

1. Dribble forward slowly (diagram 1)
2. After stopping the ball with the sole of the foot take it off again quickly, don't let the players jump off the top of the ball! (diagram 2)
3. Jump over the ball with both feet landing side on with the outside of the right foot furthest forward and the outside left foot nearest the ball. As if standing on a surf board (diagram 3)
4. Use the outside of the left foot to kick through the centre of the ball knocking it back the way the player came from (diagram 4)

Coaching Older Players

1. The players should imagine a defender ahead of them. This shows the reason for jumping over the ball and trying to get the body between the ball and the defender ahead of them.
2. Once the player has jumped over the ball encourage the player to move their arm up to hold off the player ahead of them.

Drill - Dribbling Gates

Organization

A 20 x 20 yard square is marked out and filled with a series of gates made up of two marker cones (more gates than players). All the players are given a ball.

Description

The players try to dribble the ball around the square going through as many of the cone gates or goals they can. The players should use all parts of both feet taking small touches to dribble the ball keeping it as close as possible.

Coaching Points to Improve Dribbling in this drill.

1. Attitude - Be positive at all times the player should always believe they will get past a defender or keep control of the ball.
2. Approach - The approach should be controlled and thoughtful. The player should not look down at the ball but ahead of it so they can see both the ball and the way ahead.
3. Decision - The player needs to make a clear decision early, where are they going next and how do they get there.
4. Contact - The contact depends on where the player wants to go.
5. Exploit the space - After getting through a gate the player should accelerate away as in a game where they would try to leave a defender unable to recover.

Progressions and Drill Variations

For Younger Players.

1. Add more gates or bigger gates.
2. Give them lots of time to achieve lots of gates and success to breed confidence.

For Older or Better Players.

1. Less gates or smaller gates.
2. Challenge them, how many gates in short time periods?

Fun

Split the group into pairs. One player starts with the ball and tries to dribble through as many goals as possible while the other player tries to win the ball off them and reverse the roles. Which of the players gains 10 goals or gates first. Rotate the player starting with the ball.

End Game - Wing Gates Game

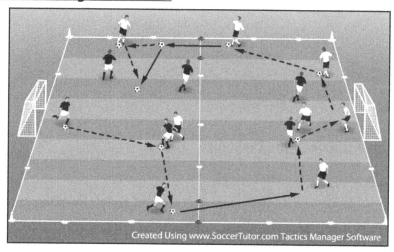

Created Using www.SoccerTutor.com Tactics Manager Software

Organization

A 60 x 40 yard pitch is marked out with four traffic cones in the corners and marker cones all around. You may need to change the size of the pitch to make it more suitable to the size and power of your players. Place two marker cone gates at the edges of the half way line, use different colour cones to mark these goals / gates.

Description

In this tactical game the sides line up with a goalkeeper, four defenders and two attackers. The only way the ball can get from the defenders to the attackers is via a defender dribbling the ball across the half way line through one of the wide gates. The player can then join with the attackers to try and score before rejoining the defence.

Progressions and Drill Variations

For Younger Players

1. Use wider gates.
2. Put the gate in a wide channel so no other players can tackle or get in the way.

For Older Players

1. Use smaller gates.

Fun

Keep the scores and add competition. Give the teams a bonus goal every time they dribble through the gate.

Question and Coach the Players?

What can you coach?
1. The dribbling player needs to see around them so make sure they don't just look at the ball. Can they control the ball and look ahead of the ball.
2. Make sure the players use both feet and all parts to keep the ball under control.

End the session by removing the half way line and the gates. The players can now finish the session playing a standard game of soccer.

Session 7 - Shooting

Session Objective	Shooting - Coach to Improve Accurate Shooting
Duration	1 Hour
Equipment	First Aid Kit, Mobile Phone, Ball for each Player, 2x sets of Bibs, Disc Marker Cones, 14x Traffic Cones, 2x Target Goals, Ball Pump, Whistle, Register.

Warm Up - Ball Work

Organization

Always begin with the same warm up within the 20x20 yard coned square. The warm up should consist of Jogging, forward, backward and sideways movement, knees up and bum kicks, hoping, skipping and jumping.

Progression - Ball Work - "360 Degree Spin"

The players have one ball each and dribble about within the square using both feet, inside, outside, sole and laces. In this session we want to coach the 360 degree spin.

Diagram 1

Stop the Ball with
the Sole of the Right Foot

Diagram 2

Spin Around 180 Degrees.
The Player now Facing Backwards
puts the sole of the Left Foot on the Ball
and the Right Foot Next to the Ball.

The Left Foot Drags the Ball Backwards Before the Player Continues to Spin Through Another 180 Degrees

The Player is now Facing Forward Again and Continues to Dribble the Ball Away with Both Feet.

To start the spin the players dribble the ball forward before stopping the ball with the sole of the foot (in this case the right foot) The player then starts to spin placing their right foot next to the ball with the toes facing backward and their left foot on the ball, heal facing forward (the player is now facing backwards). The player then drags the ball back with the sole of the left foot before continuing the spin to face forward again and continue dribbling. The players should practice the "Spin" turning both ways.

Coaching Younger Players

When coaching the very young players for the first time demonstrate each of the four steps slowly and in the logical order below.

1. Dribble forward slowly and then stop the ball with the sole of the foot (diagram 1).
2. The player takes their right foot off again quickly and starts to spin placing their right foot next to the ball with the toes facing backward and their left foot on the ball, heal facing forward, the player is now facing backwards (diagram 2).
3. The player then drags the ball back with the sole of the left foot, this in fact sends the ball in the original forward direction (diagram 3)
4. The player then continues the spin to face forward again and continue dribbling (diagram 4)

Coaching Older Players

1. The players should try and put together the four individual steps and perform the turn in one complete movement.

2. Can they perform the movement with the smallest movement of the ball prior to continuing the dribble.

Give the players a couple of minutes to dribble about practising their skills.

Drill - Accurate Shooting

Created Using www.SoccerTutor.com Tactics Manager Software

Organization

The players are split into pairs with one ball between them to use and one ball (the target ball) placed on a cone in the middle of them. The idea of the drill is for the players in each team to knock the target ball off the central marker cone.

Description

On the coaches command "shoot" all the players on one side take their shots trying to knock the target ball off the cone. The balls can then be collected by the other player in the pair while the coach resets any target balls that have been knocked off. Only when all the balls are replaced and everyone is ready should the coach shout "shoot" for the second player's to have their attempt. The drill can then repeat.

Coaching Points to Improve Shooting in this drill.

1. Approach – Take a couple of steps moving onto the ball slightly from the side.

2. Body Shape - The standing foot should be planted next to the ball with the toes pointing towards the target ball whilst allowing space for the kicking foot to swing through. The head should be steady, knee over the ball and arms out for balance.
3. Contact – The laces of the boot should contact through the centre of the ball.
4. Follow through - A short follow through to keep the ball down and accurate.

Progressions and Drill Variations

For Younger Players.

1. Make the distance between the players and target balls smaller.

For Older or Better Players.

1. Make the distance longer.
2. Use smaller target balls.

Fun

Split the players on each side into teams. How many balls are knocked off by each team. Which team scores the most goals (knocks off the most balls)

End Game - Accurate Shooting Game

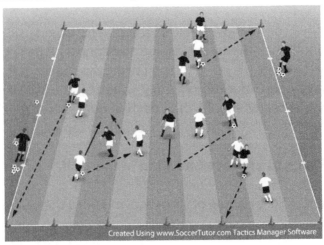

Created Using www.SoccerTutor.com Tactics Manager Software

Organization

A 20x20 yard square is set up with marker cones along two sides and five traffic cones along each of the two ends. All the players are split into two teams. The object being to try and knock over the traffic cones at the opponents end of the pitch.

Description

The coach starts the game by rolling a ball into the square. The assistants also add balls, try to keep 3 or 4 balls in play all the time. The teams compete to win a ball and shoot to knock over one of the traffic cones at the opposite end of the pitch.

Progressions and Drill Variations

For Younger Players

1. Use larger goals and more of them.

For Older Players

1. Use less cones or smaller cones.
2. Mark out an area the players are not allowed to enter at each end so the players have to shoot from further away.

Fun

Keep the scores and add competition with the first team to knock over five cones winning. Adding extra balls will add to the chaos, speed and fun of knocking over more cones. Add extra balls at anytime.

Small Sided Game

Organization

To use this drill as a small sided game simply reduce the teams to four a side. Use one ball at a time to promote passing and accurate shooting. A "No Go" end zone can also be introduced for the better players if required.

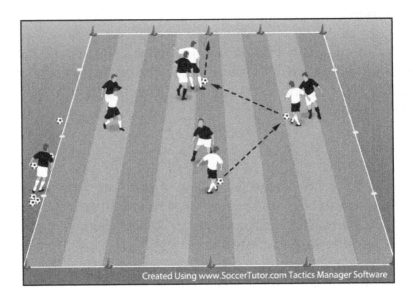

Created Using www.SoccerTutor.com Tactics Manager Software

Question and Coach the Players?

Accurate Shooting?

1. When the players are near to the target cones should they shoot with their laces? No Just like slotting a ball past an advancing keeper or into an unguarded net the player should use the inside of the foot. The shot becomes a short accurate pass.
2. When the player is further away they should use their laces to increase the power and combine this with the accuracy.
3. Did the player make the correct choice and play the best type of shot?
4. Use the coaching points to explain, demonstrate and coach accurate shooting.

End the session by extending the area and removing the traffic cones. Add the goals to the ends and the players can now finish the session playing a standard game of soccer.

Session 8 - Heading

Session Objective	Heading - Coach to Improve Heading
Duration	1 Hour
Equipment	First Aid Kit, Mobile Phone, Ball for each Player, 2 x sets of Bibs, Disc Marker Cones, 4 x Traffic Cones, 2 x Target Goals, Ball Pump, Whistle, Register.

Warm Up - Ball Work

Organization

Always begin with the same warm up within the 20x20 yard coned square. The warm up should consist of Jogging, forward, backward and sideways movement, knees up and bum kicks, hoping, skipping and jumping.

Progression - Ball Work - "Outside Hook" Turn

The players have one ball each and dribble about within the square using both feet, inside, outside, sole and laces. In this session we want to coach the "Outside Hook".

Diagram 1
Dribble the Ball
Forward Using both Feet

Diagram 2
The Player Stretches thier Right Foot
Beyond the Ball and then plays it Back
with the Outside of the Right Foot

Diagram 3
Now the Player can Turn and Push
Off the Left Foot to Accelerate Away
in the Direction they Came.

The players start by dribbling the ball forward before reaching out and in front of the ball with the foot (in this case the right foot) The outside of the foot then knocks the ball backwards for the player to turn and take the ball away in the opposite direction. The players should practice the "Outside Hook" turn using both their right and left feet.

Coaching Younger Players

When coaching the very young players for the first time break each of the three steps down and explain them in the logical order.

1. Dribble forward slowly (diagram 1)
2. Reach beyond the ball with the outside of the foot contacting with the centre of the front of the ball (diagram 2).
3. The player can now turn to the right following the ball to dribble it away back in the direction they have just come from (diagram 3)

Coaching Older Players

1. The players should try the "Outside Hook" with the left foot as well as the right. Simply reach out and beyond the ball with the left foot, turning to the left to knock the ball back.
2. Encourage the player to keep their body between any defender and the ball.

Give the players a couple of minutes to dribble about practising their skills.

Drill - Heading

Organization

The players are split into pairs with one ball between them. The players stand roughly 5ft apart dependant upon the skill and age of the players.

Description

The players take turns heading the ball to each other. The first player throws the ball up and then heads it across to their partner who then repeats heading the ball back. The drill then repeats with the players heading the ball to each other.

Coaching Points to Improve Heading in this drill.

1. Approach – The players should be steady and always watching the ball.
2. Body Shape - The players should have their eyes open and mouths closed, so they don't shut their mouths on their tongues when they head the ball.
3. Contact – The forehead should contact through the centre of the underneath of the ball to head up and away (defensive header) or through the centre of the top of the ball to head down (attacking header).

Progressions and Drill Variations

For Younger Players.

1. Make the distance between the players smaller.
2. To start with have the players kneeling down or maybe heading out of their hands to gain confidence.

For Older or Better Players.

1. Make the distance further.
2. Instead of throwing the ball up for themselves to head have the partner throw the ball up for them to head the ball back, have three goes each before swapping.

Fun

Build the confidence and always finish with a diving header, all the players no matter what age love diving in the mud for a header.

End Game - Attacking Wingers Game

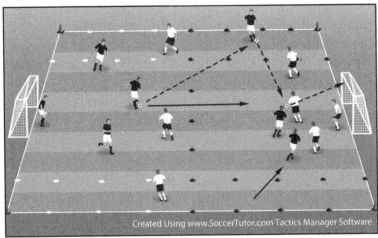

Organization

A 60 x 40 yard pitch is marked out with four traffic cones in the corners and marker cones all around. You may need to change the size of the pitch to make it more suitable to the size and power of your players. Place marker cones along each side of the pitch to create channels, approximately 5 foot wide and also add a half way line.

Description

In this tactical game the sides line up with a goalkeeper, three defenders and one attacker. The teams also have two attacking wingers, one positioned in each of the wing channels in the attacking half of the pitch. No other player can enter these channels. The only way the ball can get from the defenders to the attacker is via one of these attacking wingers. The winger receives the ball from a defender and then crosses the ball into the attacker. The defender playing the ball forward can enter the attacking half to support the attack. Also, as the first winger receives the ball the second winger opposite is allowed to sprint out of their wing channel to support the attack. This gives three attackers against three defenders. Can the winger cross the ball for the attackers to head at goal?

End Game Variations

If you are short of a few players then the 3v1 in each half could be reduced to a 2v1 and instead of four wingers we can use two neutral wingers. The neutral wingers should move directly into the attacking half as soon as the defending team wins possession of the ball. We can also incorporate small target goals when we are short of a goalkeeper.

Question and Coach the Players?

Where does the winger need to cross the ball?

1. The ball should be crossed in front of the striker for them to run onto.
2. The ball should be crossed at head height or higher to enable them to practice their heading.

What else can you coach in the game?

3. The attackers should head the ball down at the ground to optimize the chance of scoring, try hitting the goal line with the ball by heading above the centre of the ball with the forehead.
4. The defenders should also try to head the ball. They should contact the underside of the ball with the forehead, heading it up and as far away as possible.

End the session by removing the channels so the players can play normally.

Important Note

Don't let the players continue heading endlessly limit the number of headers and the power of them.

Session 9 - Turns

Session Objective	Turns - Coach to Improve Turning with the Ball
Duration	1 Hour
Equipment	First Aid Kit, Mobile Phone, Ball for each Player, 2 x sets of Bibs, Disc Marker Cones, 4 x Traffic Cones, 2 x Target Goals, Ball Pump, Whistle, Register.

Warm Up - Ball Work

Organization

Always begin with the same warm up within the 20x20 yard coned square. The warm up should consist of Jogging, forward, backward and sideways movement, knees up and bum kicks, hoping, skipping and jumping.

Created Using www.SoccerTutor.com Tactics Manager Software

In this warm up square we have added a series of single marker cones dotted all around the square. Ask the players to dribble about within the square as normal but challenge them to dribble around the cones, this makes them start to turn with the ball. You may want to add these cones whenever the progression is a particular technical skill that can be practised turning around a cone or by using the cone as a defender.

Progression - Ball Work - "Step Over" Turn

The players have one ball each and dribble about within the square using both feet, inside, outside, sole and laces. In this session we want to coach the "Step Over" turn.

Dribble the Ball
Forward Using both Feet

The Player Pretends to Kick the Ball with the Right Foot but Goes Over the Ball and Plants the Foot Diagonally Ahead.

Pivoting on the Right Foot the Player Swings the Left Foot all the Way Round to Take the Ball Away with the Instep

Now The Player can Turn and Dribble the Ball Back in the Direction they Came.

The players start by dribbling the ball forward before pretending the kick the ball (to the left with the right foot in this case) The players foot should plant down diagonally opposite its starting position and over the ball. The body then spins round (in this case turning right) pivoting on this foot. The ball is then taken away backwards with the instep of the other foot (in this case the left foot) The players should practice the "Step Over" turn using both their right and left feet.

Coaching Younger Players

When coaching the very young players for the first time break each of the four steps down and explain them in the logical order.

1. Dribble forward slowly (diagram 1)
2. Pretend to kick the ball but swing the foot beyond the front of the ball and place it diagonally opposite its starting position (diagram 2).
3. The player can now spin, pivoting on the ball of this foot round in the other direction so the instep of the other foot can contact through the centre of the ball (diagram 3)
4. The player can now take the ball away backwards (diagram 4)

Coaching Older Players

1. The players should use the first kick to try and fool the defender into thinking they are really going to strike the ball. The player should swing their arms and body to exaggerate the kick.
2. Encourage the players to try the "Step Over" turning both ways, using both feet.

Give the players a couple of minutes to dribble about practising their skills.

Drill - Turns - Small Sided Game

Created Using www.SoccerTutor.com Tactics Manager Software

Organization

Four traffic cones mark out a 20x20 square. The players are split into two teams of four players with two players from each team standing on opposite ends of the square. The other two players work within the square.

Description

One player starts with the ball and the purpose of the drill is to pass the ball via at least one of their team mates in the square to the receiver on the opposite side of the square. The other team tries to win the ball and do the same, passing the ball across the square from a player on one side to their receiver on the other.

Coaching Points to Improve Turns in this drill.

1. Approach - The approach should be controlled moving forward with the ball.
2. Protection - The player should use their legs and body to protect the ball. Always turn away from the defender and never into them.
3. Body Shape - The player should be well balanced, knees bent and arms out for balance with the head steady.
4. Technique - The technique of the turn, was it executed correctly?
5. Exploit the space - After executing a turn the player should accelerate away leaving any defender unable to recover.

Progressions and Drill Variations

For Younger Players.

1. Make the square bigger.

For Older or Better Players.

1. Make the square smaller.
2. Play 3 V 3 within the square.

Fun

Challenge the two teams awarding a goal for each successful pass across the square via a player in the middle. Which team can complete five passes and get to five goals first?

End Game - Thirds Turning Game

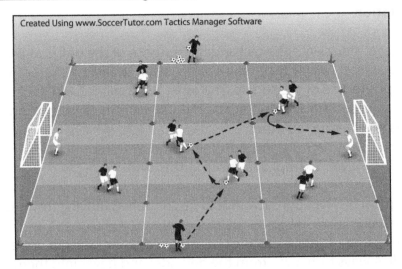

Created Using www.SoccerTutor.com Tactics Manager Software

Organization

A 50 x 30 yard pitch is marked out with four traffic cones in the corners and marker cones all around. You may need to change the size of the pitch to make it more suitable to the size and power of your players. Place marker cones across the pitch to split it into three thirds.

Description

In this tactical game each team starts with two players in each third, essentially a two v two. The players cannot move from their designated third. Each team can attack both ends and score in either goal. The players in the midfield receive a ball from the coach and twist and turn trying to find a team mate in either end zone who can receive the ball and get in a shot.

End Game Variations

If you are short of a few players then reduce the players in each third. Keep at least a 2v2 in the midfield as shown and then reduce to a 1v1 in each end zone. You could also go to a 3v3 in the midfield zone if required. If you do you may want to vary the size of each third accordingly.

Question and Coach the Players?

How can we use this end game to help coach our players?

1. Each player needs to tell the player with the ball where they are and where they want the ball. Communication is the key especially when the player with the ball is facing the opposite direction.
2. Can the player with the ball change the direction of the attack. Start attacking one goal then turn and attack the other.

End the session by removing the thirds leaving a standard pitch. The players can now finish the session playing a normal game.

Session 10 - Dribbling

Session Objective   Turns - Coach to Improve Dribbling with the Ball.

Duration   1 Hour

Equipment   First Aid Kit, Mobile Phone, Ball for each Player, 2 x sets of Bibs, Disc Marker Cones, 4 x Traffic Cones, 2 x Target Goals, Ball Pump, Whistle, Register.

Warm Up - Ball Work

Organization

Always begin with the same warm up within the 20x20 yard coned square. The warm up should consist of Jogging, forward, backward and sideways movement, knees up and bum kicks, hoping, skipping and jumping.

Progression - Ball Work - "Mathews" Move

The players have one ball each and dribble about within the square using both feet, inside, outside, sole and laces. In this session we want to coach the "Mathews" move.

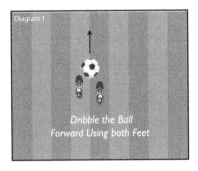
Diagram 1
Dribble the Ball Forward Using both Feet

Diagram 2
Knock the Ball to the Left with the Inside of the Right Foot Twice.

Diagram 3

The Player then Uses the Outside of the Right Foot to Play the Ball Back to the Right and Diagonally Forward

Diagram 4

The Player can then Sprint into this Space Created by moving the Defender to the Left.

The players start by dribbling the ball forward before knocking the ball to the side (in this case to the left with the inside of the right foot) The player takes two touches knocking it to the side before knocking the ball back the other way and forward (in this case with the outside of the right foot) The players should practice the "Mathews" move going both ways and therefore using both their right and left feet.

Coaching Younger Players

When coaching the very young players for the first time break each of the four steps down and explain them in the logical order.

1. Dribble forward slowly (diagram 1)
2. Kick the ball twice to the side with the instep of the foot (diagram 2).
3. The player can now knock the ball back and forward with the outside of the same foot (diagram 3)
4. The player can now take the ball away in that direction (diagram 4)

Coaching Older Players

1. The players should imagine drawing a defender across to the side as they knock the ball across. Moving the defender creates a space where they were for the dribbling player to exploit and move into.
2. The player should sprint away into the space and beyond leaving any defender struggling to get back to challenge.

Give the players a couple of minutes to dribble about practising their skills.

Drill - Dribbling Cones

Created Using www.SoccerTutor.com Tactics Manager Software

Organization

Marker cones are used to set out a slalom course for the players to dribble around. The slalom course consists of five cones with one centrally at each end to mark the starts. The three in the middle are set two paces apart and also one pace off the centre line to the side as shown. The players are split into teams and each team have half the players at one end of the slalom and the others at the other end.

Description

The first player in the line starts with the ball and dribbles it through the slalom before passing it to the first player in the opposite line. The new player then dribbles the ball back while the first player joins the back of the line. The drill can then continue.

Coaching Points to Improve Dribbling in this drill.

1. Attitude - The player must always believe in their ability and be positive and comfortable on the ball.
2. Contact - the player should contact the centre of the ball keeping it moving straight and along the floor.

3. Technique - Small touches! Players will not go faster by taking bigger kicks they just have more chance of loosing control in these tight areas.
4. End Product - The final pass to the next player needs to be to feet and at a pace that is easy to control.

Progressions and Drill Variations

For Younger Players.

1. Make the course straight and make the spacing between the cones bigger.
2. Challenge the two teams, which team is the first to have all its players complete the course.

For Older or Better Players.

1. Make the spacing smaller and add more cones.
2. Remove the cones and challenge the players to dribble in a confined space.

Created Using www.SoccerTutor.com Tactics Manager Software

Organization

Use a small 5x5 square set out with marker cones and traffic cones as shown.

Description

Split the players into two teams. Give each player from one of the teams a ball and get them to dribble about inside the small square. The other team waits around the square. The players in the square must try to dribble as fast as they can keeping the ball within the square. After 30 seconds or so swap the teams working in the square.

Progressions and Drill Variations

For Younger Players.

1. Make the square bigger.

For Older or Better Players.

1. Make the square smaller.
2. Challenge the two teams to compete against each other, which team is dribbles the fastest? Which team keeps the ball within the square?

End Game - Thirds Dribbling Game

Created Using www.SoccerTutor.com Tactics Manager Software

Organization

A 50 x 30 yard pitch is marked out with four traffic cones in the corners and marker cones all around. You may need to change the size of the pitch to make it more suitable to the size and power of your players. Place marker cones across the pitch to split it into three thirds.

Description

In this tactical game each team starts with a goalkeeper, two defenders, three midfielders and a striker. All the players stick to their third except the midfielders who are given the option to move into the attacking third. The rule is only one midfielder can move into the final third at any one time and the only way they can move in is to dribble in with the ball.

End Game Variations

With very young or inexperienced players you may want to start with a pitch split simply into two halves. See variations in the extra drills section of the book. The same game can be played with a single player from the defensive half dribbling into the attacking half. The two halves should be set up with a 3v2 where 3 defenders are up against 2 attackers.

Question and Coach the Players?

How can we use this end game to help coach our players?

1. Each midfielder needs to be positive and attack the final third if they have the chance by dribbling into it or at a defender.
2. Create space and keep the head up so the players can receive the ball in a position where they can attack or dribble forward.
3. Praise any dribbling or attempt to take on an opponent but remember to highlight success and what made it successful.

End the session by removing the thirds leaving a standard pitch. The players can now finish the session playing a normal game.

Session 11 - Goalkeeping

Session Objective	Goalkeeping - Coach to Improve Handling.

Duration	1 Hour

Equipment	First Aid Kit, Mobile Phone, Ball for each Player, 2 x sets of Bibs, Disc Marker Cones, 4 x Traffic Cones, 2 x Target Goals, Ball Pump, Whistle, Register.

Warm Up - Ball Work

Organization

Always begin with the same warm up within the 20x20 yard coned square. The warm up should consist of Jogging, forward, backward and sideways movement, knees up and bum kicks, hoping, skipping and jumping.

Progression - Ball Work - Handling

Created Using www.SoccerTutor.com Tactics Manager Software

The players pick the ball up and move about within the square. They should sidestep around the square keeping the ball in front of their body. Can the players keep their feet as close to the floor as possible as they move about.

The players introduce bouncing and catching the ball. Can they bounce the ball with both hands and catch with both hands in the "W" position in front of their body.

The players can also throw the ball up into the air and jump up to catch. Can they jump high to catch the ball as high as possible again with the "W" hand shape. Can they jump off their right leg only and then try jumping just off their left leg.

Drill - Goalkeeping

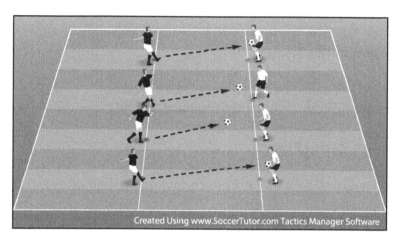

Created Using www.SoccerTutor.com Tactics Manager Software

Organization

The players are split into pairs with one ball between them. The players stand roughly 5ft apart dependant upon the skill and age of the players.

Description

The players take turns throwing the ball to each other. The first player throws the ball across to their partner who should catch the ball they can then roll the ball back and the drill continues. The players should start rolling the ball along the ground to each other. They should then throw the ball into the players waist. They can then throw head height and then throw up for their partner to jump up and catch.

Coaching Points to Improve Goalkeeping in this drill.

1. Approach – The players should be steady and always watching the ball.
2. Body Shape - The players should have their feet placed shoulder width apart and be leaning slightly forward waiting to receive the ball.
3. Contact – The players should scoop the ball up into their arms when rolled along the floor or thrown toward their waist. Any higher and the player should use the "W" where their hands and fingers are splayed upwards and open with the thumbs almost touching

Progressions and Drill Variations

For Younger Players.

1. Make the distance between the players shorter.
2. Make sure the throws are not too hard and fast.

For Older or Better Players.

1. The players should move from throwing the ball onto kicking it to their partner.
2. Make the distance further.

Fun

Finish the drill with some diving shots or throws to save.

<u>End Game - Goalkeeping Shot Stopping.</u>

Organization

A 20x30 yard rectangle is set out with marker cones. You may need to change the size of the pitch to make it more suitable to the size and power of your players. Place two marker cones at the midway point on the sides of the rectangle. Two goals are positioned centrally, one at each end. Four balls are needed and placed one at each corner.

Created Using www.SoccerTutor.com Tactics Manager Software

Description

The two goalkeepers take their positions one in each goal. Six players are positioned around the area, one at each corner and two centrally on either side. All these players are given a number.

The drill starts with the player in the top left hand corner (number 1) shooting at the goalkeeper in the goal opposite. Once this shot is saved, goal scored or goes wide the player in the bottom left corner (number 3) takes their shot at the other goalie opposite them. All the four corner players take their turn shooting (order 1,3,4,6) All the players then move round one position including the goalkeepers. The player number 3 becomes the opposite goalkeeper, that goalkeeper becomes the bottom goalkeeper who moves to become player 4. Player 6 becomes player 1.

For Older or Better Players.

1. The players in positions 2 and 4 should react all of the shots and chase them in to add pressure on the keepers.
2. The goalkeepers shoot at their opponent goalkeeper should they catch the ball or gather it cleanly. The drill can then continue with the goalkeepers shooting at each other until the ball goes dead, for example a goal is scored or the ball goes wide.

3. Speed up the drill by letting the next corner player shoot as soon as the ball goes dead.

Fun

Which goalkeeper keeps the most clean sheets, keep score adding competition.

End Game Variations

If you are short of a few players then remove the two middle players (2 and 5). If you have a couple of extra players position them behind the goals to collect balls shot wide. These players then take the place of the goalkeepers when everyone moves around.

Question and Coach the Players?

How can we use this end game to help coach our players?

1. Did the goalkeeper make the correct save? Did they get their body behind the ball? Did they catch the ball using the "W" or did they scoop it up correctly?
2. Did the central players close down the goalkeeper? Did they react to the shot or the rebound? Always chase in the shot do not wait for the rebound.
3. Did the player get their original shot on target? Did they shoot with their laces? Did they keep the ball down?
4. Did the goalkeeper get back into their set position as quickly as possible to be ready the next shot?

End the session by letting the players play a normal game.

Session 12 - Long Lofted Passing

Session Objective Passing - Coach to Improve Players Long Passing

---

Duration 1 Hour

Equipment First Aid Kit, Mobile Phone, Ball for each Player, 2 x sets of Bibs, Disc Marker Cones, 4 x Traffic Cones, 2 x Target Goals, Ball Pump, Whistle, Register.

Warm Up - Ball Work

Organization

Always begin with the same warm up within the 20x20 yard coned square. The warm up should consist of Jogging, forward, backward and sideways movement, knees up and bum kicks, hoping, skipping and jumping.

Progression - Ball Work - "Inside Hook" Turn

The players have one ball each and dribble about within the square using both feet, inside, outside, sole and laces. In this session we want to coach the "Inside Hook".

The players start by dribbling the ball forward before reaching out and in front of the ball with the foot (in this case the right foot) The inside of the foot then knocks the ball backwards for the player to turn and take the ball away in the opposite direction. The players should practice the "Inside Hook" turn using both their right and left feet.

Coaching Younger Players

When coaching the very young players for the first time break each of the three steps down and explain them in the logical order.

1. Dribble forward slowly (diagram 1)
2. Reach beyond the ball with the inside of the foot contacting with the centre of the front of the ball (diagram 2).
3. The player can now turn to the left following the ball to dribble it away back in the direction they have just come from (diagram 3)

Coaching Older Players

1. The players should try the "Inside Hook" with the left foot as well as the right. Simply reach out and beyond the ball with the left foot, turning to the right to knock the ball back with the inside of the foot.
2. Encourage the player to keep their body between any defender and the ball.

Give the players a couple of minutes to dribble about practising their skills.

Drill - Long Lofted Passing

Created Using www.SoccerTutor.com Tactics Manager Software

Organization

The players are split into pairs with one ball between them. Cones mark out two lines roughly 20ft apart. The players stand facing each other next to the cones. The 20ft spacing is dependant upon the strength and age of the players.

Description

The players take turns lofting the ball to each other. The first player passes the ball across to their partner who should control it. The other player can then place the ball take a few steps back and take their turn lofting the pass back, the drill can then repeat.

Coaching Points to Improve Long Lofted Passing in this drill.

1. Approach - The player approaches the ball slightly from the side.
2. Body shape - The standing foot should be slightly back from the side of the ball resulting in the kicking foot slightly reaching for the ball.
3. Contact - The top of the foot, a little above the big toe, contacts with the underside of the middle of the ball.
4. Follow through - A big and high follow through with the kicking foot to gain height and power.

Progressions and Drill Variations

For Younger Players.

1. Make the distance between the players shorter.

For Older or Better Players.

1. Add a player in the middle that they need to loft the ball over.
2. Make the distance further.

Fun

Piggy in the middle. If the players on the edge cannot lift the ball over the middle player they swap places.

End Game - Four Zone Passing Game.

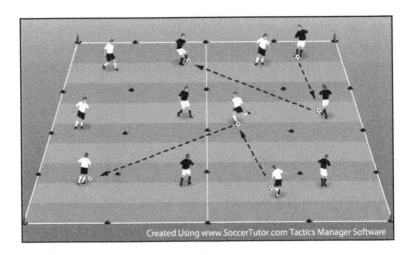

Organization

A 50 x 30 yard pitch is marked out with four traffic cones in the corners and marker cones all around. The pitch is then split into four strips using more marker cones. You may need to change the size of the pitch to make it more suitable to the size and power of your players.

Description

In this small sided game we split the players into two teams and these teams are split equally into two of the four zones (not next to each other) In our diagram we see two teams of six players split with three players in each of their zones. The idea is for a team to pass the ball from their end zone through or over the adjacent opponents zone and to a teammate in their central zone.

Progressions and Drill Variations

For Younger Players.

1. Allow all types of passes.
2. Make the zones thin to enable shorter lofted passes.

For Older or Better Players.

1. Make the zones wider to increase the length of pass and height required.
2. Challenge the players to make a driven pass through the opposing team to a team mate in the other zone.

Fun

Keep score with each team gaining a goal for a successful pass from one zone to the other.

End Game Variations

If you are short of a few players then reduce the players in each zone.

<u>Question and Coach the Players?</u>

Can we promote Longer lofted passing?

1. Use the full width and length of the pitch and get into a position where the player with the ball can pass to you.
2. Can the players pass within the zones switching the play from one side to the other to work an opening for a pass across?

End the session by removing the zones and adding goals to create a standard pitch. The players can now finish the session playing a game.

**To compliment this training program use the
UK's number 1 best selling skills and coaching football book.**

Coaching The Coach
A Complete guide how to coach soccer skills through drills.

The sole objective of "Coaching The Coach" is to educate and improve all new football coaches. Written in a completely unique question and answer style, it expands on why you choose a drill, how you will use it and what you will coach.

Endorsed by The Association of Football Coaches as "A fantastic coaching resource" the book can just as easily be used by parents, teachers, young sports leaders or even youth players themselves as they all seek to improve.

Jon Carter from www.ESPNsoccernet.com said in his online review "Indeed, with an easy to read, logical, and fun coaching manual like this one on the market, it should only be a matter of time before grassroots football in England begins to improve."

Dr. Jay Martin of the National Soccer Coaches Association of America (NSCAA) wrote in an article for the NSCAA official publication Soccer Journal. "Although the book is aimed at the new youth coach, any coach will get a great deal from reading this book. It is short, it has a lot of pictures and it is very good. What more do you need for a little summer reading?"

Coaching The Coach
A Complete guide how to coach soccer skills through drills.

Available from www.SoccerTutor.com

Extra Drills

The next section includes many drills which compliment the sessions. Simply swap the drill in the program with the drill you feel best fits the standard and developmental needs of the players you are coaching.

To order Coaching Software, DVDs, Books and Magazines visit www.SoccerTutor.com

Don't Forget to Register Online for free weekly emails containing more great drills, tips and offers

Extra Drill - Quick Shooting Drill
In the Box

Drill - Suitable for Ages 8-10

Created Using www.SoccerTutor.com Tactics Manager Software

Organization

A 30x30 yard square is set out using marker cones, a smaller 10x10 yard square is marked within it. Two goals are marked or target goals placed at either end of the smaller square. The players are split into two teams and they play in the larger square only. A neutral striker is placed in the central square where they stay waiting for the ball to be played into them.

Description

The drill begins with the coach introducing a ball to the players in the outside square. The two teams play against each other trying to pass the ball into the central striker who finishes the move with a shot. By using poles or traffic cones to mark the goals, when a shot is taken the game can continue as the ball is now back in the larger square and back in play with the two teams.

Coaching Points to Improve Shooting in this drill.

1. Approach – Sprint to the ball directly to get there as quickly as possible. Shoot whenever and as soon as the possibility arises.
2. Body Shape - The standing foot should be planted next to the ball with the toes pointing towards the goal whilst allowing space for the kicking foot to swing through. The head should be steady, knee over the ball and arms out for balance.
3. Contact – The shot should be taken with the foot nearest to the ball so there is no delay. The laces of the boot should contact through the centre of the ball.
4. Follow through - A short but sharp and strong follow through to keep the ball down and accurate.

Progressions and Drill Variations

For Younger Players.

1. Less players, make the game a 4v4 in the outside area.
2. Bigger goals to promote success and make scoring easier.

For Older or Better Players.

1. Smaller target goals.
2. Add goalkeepers.
3. Play a 1v1 in the centre square with two teams.

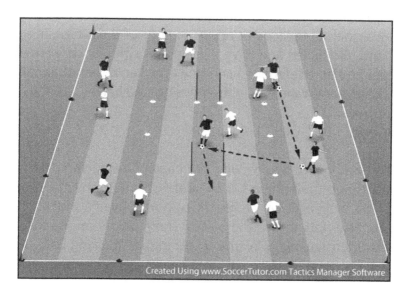

Created Using www.SoccerTutor.com Tactics Manager Software

Extra Drill - Quick Shooting Small Sided Game
Long Shots

Small Sided Game - Suitable for Ages 7-10

Created Using www.SoccerTutor.com Tactics Manager Software

Organization

A 30x30 yard square is set out using marker cones and a half way line is added. Two goals are placed at opposite ends of the pitch. The players are split into two teams and have three players in their defensive half (a goalkeeper and two defenders) and one attacker in the other half of the pitch. The players always stay in their designated halves.

Description

The small sided game begins with the coach introducing a ball to one of the teams and their players in the defensive half. This team pass the ball amongst themselves to create the opportunity of a shot at goal. The other team attempts to win the ball off them. Shots can be taken from within the defensive half or by the striker in the attacking half.

Coaching Points to Improve Shooting in this drill.

1. Approach – Pass the ball to create an opportunity and shoot whenever and as soon as the possibility arises.
2. Body Shape - The standing foot should be planted next to the ball with the toes pointing towards the goal whilst allowing space for the kicking foot to swing through. The head should be steady, knee over the ball and arms out for balance.
3. Contact – The shot should be taken with the foot nearest to the ball so there is no delay. The laces of the boot should contact through the centre of the ball.
4. Follow through - A short but sharp and strong follow through to keep the ball down and accurate.
5. End product - The shot needs to be on target and the striker should always follow in the shot for any rebounds. The strikers should chase in the shot not wait and chase after the rebound.

Progressions and Drill Variations

For Younger Players.

1. Smaller halves.
2. Bigger goals to promote success and make scoring easier.

For Older or Better Players.

1. Smaller target goals.
2. Add goalkeepers.
3. Make the pitch bigger.

Fun

Keep the score, which team wins?

End Game Variations

If you have a few more players then increase the 3v1 overload in each half to a 4v1 or even a 4v2 overload.

Extra Drill - Short Passing
New Player Introduction

Drill - Suitable for Ages 6-8

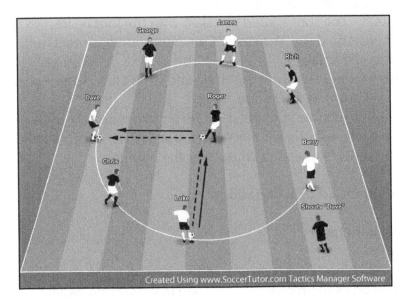

Created Using www.SoccerTutor.com Tactics Manager Software

Organization

The players form a circle with one player in the centre. The ball starts with a player on the outside circle.

Description

The drill begins with a player on the outside passing the ball into the central player. On the pass the coach shouts the name of another player standing on the outside circle. The player in the middle receives the ball and passes it out to the player called by the coach. All the players follow their pass. This means the player starting the drill becomes the middle receiving player while the middle player passing the ball out follows the pass to join the players in the circle. The players need to listen to the coach calling names so they can make their pass. This also helps introduce any new players to the team.

Coaching Points to Improve Passing in this drill.

1. Approach – Slightly from the side to give enough room to make a comfortable pass. If the player moves straight onto the ball then there is a possibility to toe poke the ball.
2. Body Shape - The standing foot should be planted next to the ball with the toes pointing in the direction of the intended pass with an open body to allow room for the side foot pass. The head should be steady and arms out for balance.
3. Contact – The instep or inside of the foot (the largest area) should contact through the centre of the ball for a pass along the ground.
4. Follow through – This helps accuracy and power. The follow through should be in line with the intended pass to keep it accurate. The more follow through the more powerful the pass.

Progressions and Drill Variations

For Younger Players.

1. Make sure the player called by the coach waves their arms and calls the name of the player in the middle.

For Older or Better Players.

1. The coach is quiet and the players on the outside call the player in the middle to receive the ball. The player shouting loudest receiving the ball.

Fun

How fast can they receive the ball and pass it off?

Extra Drill - Short Passing
Two In the Middle

Drill - Suitable for Ages 7-10

Created Using www.SoccerTutor.com Tactics Manager Software

Organization

The players are split into two teams and bibbed up. The players form a circle with two players (one from each team) in the centre. The ball starts with a player on the outside circle.

Description

The drill begins with a player on the outside passing the ball into the central player from the opposite team. That player lays the ball off to the other player in the centre (again from the opposite team). They then pass the ball out to any player on the outside again from the opposite team. All the players follow their pass which means there are always two players from opposite teams in the middle and the drill can continue.

Coaching Points to Improve Passing in this drill.

1. Approach – Slightly from the side to give enough room to make a comfortable pass. If the player moves straight onto the ball then there is a possibility to toe poke the ball.
2. Body Shape - The standing foot should be planted next to the ball with the toes pointing in the direction of the intended pass with an open body to allow room for the side foot pass. The head should be steady and arms out for balance.
3. Contact – The instep or inside of the foot (the largest area) should contact through the centre of the ball for a pass along the ground.
4. Follow through – This helps accuracy and power. The follow through should be in line with the intended pass to keep it accurate. The more follow through the more powerful the pass.

Progressions and Drill Variations

For Younger Players.

1. The players do not follow their pass but stay where they are. This means the players take turns being the two in the middle.
2. Start the players following the passes slowly allowing the players to see clearly the way the drill works.

For Older or Better Players.

1. Increase the speed of the drill and challenge the players to go faster.

Fun

How fast can they receive the ball and pass it off?

Extra Drill - Possession
All Against All

Drill - Suitable for Ages 5-10

Created Using www.SoccerTutor.com Tactics Manager Software

Organization

A 20x20 yard square is marked out with four traffic cones in the corners and marker cones all around. All the players are given a ball each to dribble about within the square.

Description

All the players try to keep possession of their ball whilst dribbling about within the square. They are also told to kick out of the square any of the other players balls should they get the opportunity.

Coaching Points to Improve Shielding the Ball.

1. Observation - The player with the ball should keep their head up so they can see and know where the other players are at all times.
2. Body Shape - The player needs to keep their body between the ball and the closest other players. Keep a long barrier when another player is really close.
3. Contact - The player should use the outside of the furthest foot from the closest other players.

4. Technique - Control the ball away from the closest players. For example if another player is to the right the player should manoeuvre the ball away to the left.

Progressions and Drill Variations

For Younger Players.

1. Make the area bigger.
2. Give a short time limit.

For Older or Better Players.

1. Make the area smaller.

Fun

Award a goal to any player who maintains possession of their ball whilst knocking out an opponents ball. Which player kicks out the most balls.

Extra Drill - Possession Small Sided Game
Team Possession

Small Sided Game - Suitable for Ages 8-10

Created Using www.SoccerTutor.com Tactics Manager Software

Organization

A 30x30 yard square is marked out with four traffic cones and marker cones, a half way line is also added. The players are split into two teams of four and each team is told to start with all four players in their own half.

Description

The ball is given to one set of four players in their half and they start to pass the ball between them. The coach then calls the name of one of the opposing team players. They are then allowed into the half to try and win the ball, a 4v1 game. As soon as they win possession of the ball they pass it into their half of the field and return to it themselves. As they return to make four players in their half the coach calls the name of a player from the other team. They then move in and attempt to win the ball back, another 4v1 game in the other half. The game can then continue.

Coaching Points to Improve Shielding the Ball.

1. Observation - The player with the ball should know where the other players are at all times either by looking or feeling.
2. Body Shape - The player keeps their body between the ball and any potential danger. Keep a long barrier when another player is close.
3. Technique - Control the ball away from the closest players. For example if another player is to the right the player should manoeuvre the ball away to the left.
4. End Product - The pass and all the coaching points associated with it.

Progressions and Drill Variations

For Younger Players.

1. Make the area bigger.

For Older or Better Players.

1. Make the area smaller.
2. The coach lets two players into the opponents half (4v2)
3. The players decide which player or players go into the opposing half based on their positions.

Fun

How long can each team keep possession of the ball? Time the length of possession for each team and challenge them to keep it longer.

Extra Drill - Running With The Ball
Running Races

Drill - Suitable for Ages 5-8

Organization

Split your players into a number of teams minimum three players in a team. Using marker cones set up a series of sprint tracks for each of the teams. Place one marker cone for where the players stand and one 20ft away to mark out where the player sprints to and turns round before sprinting back.

Description

The first player in each queue has a ball and on the coaches command runs with the ball directly at the marker cone ahead. The players then turn with the ball around the cone and run with the ball back to their team mates. They pass the ball to the next player in line or they take the ball off them and the drill continues.

Coaching Points to Improve Running With The Ball.

1. Attitude - The player needs a positive attitude and a positive first touch.
2. Head Up - The player should have their head up in between touches.
3. Contact - The laces of the nearest boot should contact through the centre of the ball. They should not break their stride pattern to always play the ball with their favoured foot.
4. End product – The final pass needs to be played in front of the next player.

Progressions and Drill Variations

For Younger Players.

1. Make the area smaller in length.

For Older or Better Players.

1. Make the area longer.
2. The first player in each team starts with a ball so you always have at least two players running. Challenge your players to be the fastest there and back.
3. Can the players sprint straight at the ball being passed to them taking a positive first touch with the nearest foot to the ball.

Fun

When we have all the team sprinting simultaneously can a team catch another up and overtake them?

Extra Drill - Running With The Ball
Break Away

Drill - Suitable for Ages 7-10

Created Using www.SoccerTutor.com Tactics Manager Software

Organization

Mark an area 50x20 using marker cones with two end zones 10x20. Split you players into two teams, a team of five attackers and two defenders. The players start with two attackers and one defender in each end zone. The other attacker starts in the middle area with a ball.

Description

The drill starts with the player in the middle running with the ball toward one of the end zones. They then pass the ball off to either of the two attackers in the end zone. That attacker then breaks out of their end zone and runs with the ball across the pitch to the other end zone. The player can then pass the ball to another attacker in that end zone. The player making the pass joins the end zone they passed into. The two defenders should try and make it hard for the running players to make their pass and promote the attackers finding space for the pass.

Coaching Points to Improve Running With The Ball.

1. Attitude - The player needs to have a positive attitude, finding space away from the defender to receive the pass and then take a positive first touch to get out of the end zone.
2. Head Up - The player should have their head up in between touches so they can see the movement of the attackers in the end zones.
3. Contact - The laces of the nearest boot should contact through the centre of the ball. They should not break their stride pattern to always play the ball with their favoured foot.
4. End product – The final pass needs to be played to the player in space and in front of them so they can sprint onto the pass.

Progressions and Drill Variations

For Younger Players.

1. Make the area smaller in length.
2. Play 3v1 in each end zone to make finding another player to pass to easier.
3. Make the defenders passive.

For Older or Better Players.

1. Make the area longer.
2. Make the defenders more aggressive trying to cut out the passes.
3. Play 3v2 in the end zones to make it more difficult to find a pass.

Fun

The defender who cuts out a pass or stops the attackers becomes the attacker and the attacker loosing the ball becomes the defender.

Extra Drill - Passing
Pass, Receive, Turn

Drill - Suitable for Ages 5-8

Created Using www.SoccerTutor.com Tactics Manager Software

Organization

Marker cones are laid out to form channels in which three players can work. The channels can be 20x10 and the marker cones down the side of the channel should be placed in the middle and 5ft from each end to mark a no go end zone. The three players stand one at each end and one working in the middle.

Description

The drill begins with the player in the middle dribbling the ball toward a player at the end. Before they get to the final marker cone, 5ft away, they pass the ball to them and receive the ball back in a one-two. The player then turns to dribble the ball to the opposite end and again plays a one-two with the player at the other end. The drill continues for a set time and then the player in the middle is swapped.

Coaching Points to Improve Passing in this drill.

1. Approach – Slightly from the side to give enough room to make a comfortable pass. If the player moves straight onto the ball then there is a possibility to toe poke the ball.
2. Body Shape - The standing foot should be planted next to the ball with the toes pointing in the direction of the intended pass with an open body to allow room for the side foot pass. The head should be steady and arms out for balance.
3. Contact – The instep or inside of the foot (the largest area) should contact through the centre of the ball for a pass along the ground.
4. Follow through – This helps accuracy and power. The follow through should be in line with the intended pass to keep it accurate. The more follow through the more powerful the pass.

Progressions and Drill Variations

For Younger Players.

1. Make the end zone smaller, so the pass is over a shorter distance.
2. Make the time they work for short, 30 seconds for example.

For Older or Better Players.

1. Make the channel longer and promote longer passes.
2. Can the central players receive the ball on the half turn.
3. Introduce a specific turn each time they receive the ball

Fun

How many shuttles with complete passes can they perform in the set time?

Extra Drill - Passing
Pass and Move

Drill - Suitable for Ages 8-10

Created Using www.SoccerTutor.com Tactics Manager Software

Organization

Marker cones are used to make two squares a 10x10 inside a 20x20. Two marker cones are placed 5ft apart as goals in the centre of each side on the larger square. Four players work in the central smaller square while four other players stand within the 5ft goals on the larger square. Each of the players in the goals start with a ball.

Description

The drill starts with the four central players standing opposite the goals on the edge of the smaller square. The outer players pass the ball into them and receive the ball back. The players in the middle then sprint off within the central square to find another player on the outside who is standing with a ball waiting to make a pass. The drill continues for a set time and then the players on the outside are switched with the players on the inside.

Coaching Points to Improve Passing in this drill.

1. Approach – Slightly from the side to give enough room to make a comfortable pass. If the player moves straight onto the ball then there is a possibility to toe poke the ball.
2. Body Shape - The standing foot should be planted next to the ball with the toes pointing in the direction of the intended pass with an open body to allow room for the side foot pass. The head should be steady and arms out for balance.
3. Contact – The instep or inside of the foot (the largest area) should contact through the centre of the ball for a pass along the ground.
4. Follow through – This helps accuracy and power. The follow through should be in line with the intended pass to keep it accurate. The more follow through the more powerful the pass.

Progressions and Drill Variations

For Younger Players.

1. Make the outside square smaller, so the pass is over a shorter distance.
2. Make the time they work for short, 30 seconds for example.

For Older or Better Players.

1. Make the outside square larger to promote longer passes.
2. Make the smaller square smaller to make movement difficult.
3. Add agility poles to the central square to increase the problem of moving about within the smaller square.

Fun

How many passes can they complete in the set time and which of the four players is the winner?

Extra Drill - Dribbling
1v1 Take Them On

Drill - Suitable for Ages 5-8

Created Using www.SoccerTutor.com Tactics Manager Software

Organization

Use marker cones to set out a 20x20 square. The players are split into teams and they line up centrally on the edge of the square opposite each other. A ball is given to the first player in one of the lines. Spare balls are placed near both teams.

Description

On the coaches command the player with the ball dribbles forward and attempts to dribble the ball over the end line of the opposite team. The first player from the opposite team comes out to meet them and tries to win possession of the ball. Should they win the ball they can dribble forward over the other end line. The drill continues with the player at the head of the line at the end the player dribbles over, the losing team. Above the drill would be won by the team in black and restart with the team in white.

Coaching Points to Improve Dribbling in this drill.

1. Attitude - Be positive at all times the player should always believe they will get past the defender.
2. Approach - The approach should be controlled and thoughtful. The player should not look down at the ball but ahead of it so they can see both the ball and the defender coming to meet them.
3. Decision - The player needs to make a clear decision early, where are they going and how will they get past the defender. Which trick or move will they use.
4. Contact - The contact depends on where the player wants to go.
5. Exploit the space - After getting past the defender the player should accelerate away and leave the defender unable to recover.

Progressions and Drill Variations

For Younger Players.

1. Make the defender passive.

For Older or Better Players.

1. Make the width of the square thinner.
2. Place Target goals at each end instead of an end zone.

Fun

Keep score each time a player is successful. Which team gets past their opponents the most?

Extra Drill - Dribbling
1v1 Team Challenge

Drill - Suitable for Ages 7-10

Created Using www.SoccerTutor.com Tactics Manager Software

Organization

Use marker cones to set out two 7x7 squares approximately 10ft from the goal and 10ft apart, making a channel leading toward the goal. Put a marker cone 5ft above the left hand square and another 5ft below the right hand square. A ball is placed next to the top marker cone. The players are split into two teams and each player is numbered. A neutral goalkeeper takes position in the goal.

Description

To start the players pass the ball amongst their teammates within their squares. The coach then shouts a number. The two players from each team who have that number sprint out of their square to play 1v1. The player in the left hand square races up, around the cone collecting the ball and dribbles it down through the channel before shooting at goal. The player from the right hand square runs down around the cone and up into the channel to defend 1 against 1.

Coaching Points to Improve Dribbling in this drill.

1. Attitude - Be positive at all times the player should always believe they will get past the defender and get a shot on target.
2. Approach - The approach should be controlled and thoughtful. The player should not look down at the ball but ahead of it so they can see both the ball and the defender coming to meet them.
3. Decision - The player needs to make a clear decision early, how will they get past the defender? Which trick or move will they use.
4. Technique - The technique in taking on and getting past the defender. Was it successful and if not why not.
5. Exploit the space - After getting past the defender the player should accelerate away and leave the defender unable to recover in order to get their shot in.
6. End product - Was the shot on target?

Progressions and Drill Variations

For Younger Players.

1. Use only the left hand square and put a cone in the channel as a defender.
2. Make the defender passive.
3. Play without a goalkeeper.

For Older or Better Players.

1. Make the width of the channel thinner.

Fun

Keep score and swap the players roles. After all the players have had a turn as the attackers swap the attackers and defenders. Each time a player is successful award a goal. Which team gets past their opponents the most?

Extra Drill - Accurate Shooting
Target Goal Shooting

Drill - Suitable for Ages 5-7

Organization

A series of marker cones are set up a suitable distance from a target goal. Use two cones of the same colour to denote 1) where the ball is placed and 2) where the players line up waiting to take their shot. The players are split into three teams and the players line up on the second cone furthest from the goal.

Description

The drill starts with the coach shouting "Shoot" at which point the first player in each line runs forward to shoot at the target goal. After the players have taken their shot they retrieve the ball and set it down on the first cone again, ready for the second players shot. The players then join the back of their team line. Again the players wait for the coaches shout before taking their shots.

Coaching Points to Improve Shooting in this drill.

1. Approach – Run forward onto the ball slightly from the side.
2. Body Shape - The standing foot should be planted next to the ball with the toes pointing towards the target goal whilst allowing space for the kicking foot to swing through. The head should be steady, knee over the ball and arms out for balance.
3. Contact – The laces of the boot should contact through the centre of the ball.
4. Follow through - A short follow through to keep the ball down and accurate.
5. End Product - The shot has to be on target and into the goal.

Progressions and Drill Variations

For Younger Players.

1. For more chances for each player to shoot, split the players into four teams with less players in each team
2. Move the ball nearer the target goal.

For Older or Better Players.

1. Smaller goals.
2. Move the balls further from the target goals.

NOTE

Do not add a goalkeeper as there will be more than one shot being taken at any one time.

Fun

Move all the teams onto the next cone so they all get a chance to shoot from all the different directions. Keep the individual teams scores, which team wins?

Extra Drill - Accurate Shooting
1v1 Shooting

Small Sided Game - Suitable for Ages 8-10

Created Using www.SoccerTutor.com Tactics Manager Software

Organization

A 40x40 yard square is set out using marker cones and a middle section of 20 yards is also marked out. Two teams of five players are split with a goalkeeper placed in goals at each end of the pitch and four players from each team in the central area.

Description

The small sided game begins with the coach introducing a ball to one of the teams. Their players play keep ball in the central third. None of the players are allowed out of the central third until the team have completed three passes. A through ball can then be played into the end zone and into the path of a team mate for them to run onto and take on the goalkeeper in a 1v1 situation. Can they place an accurate shot past the goalkeeper and into the goal

Coaching Points to Improve Shooting in this drill.

1. Approach – Sprint onto the ball directly to get there as quickly as possible.
2. Body Shape - The standing foot should be planted next to the ball with the toes pointing towards the goal whilst allowing space for the kicking foot to swing through. The head should be steady, knee over the ball and arms out for balance.
3. Contact – The shot should be taken with the foot nearest to the ball so there is no delay. The inside of the boot should contact through the centre of the ball, just as with a side foot pass.
4. Follow through - A short but sharp and strong follow through to keep the ball down and accurate.
5. End Product - The ball should be passed past the goalkeeper and into the goal.

Progressions and Drill Variations

For Younger Players.

1. Less players, make the game a 3v3 in the central area.
2. Add a floating player who plays with the team in possession to give them a numerical advantage.
3. Let the players make two passes prior to passing it into the end zone.

For Older or Better Players.

1. Smaller goals.
2. More passes prior to the killer pass into the end zone.
3. More players in a smaller central zone and a smaller end zone to rush the shot.
4. Let a defending player chase the attacker into the end zone to force the attacker to shoot early.

Fun

Keep the score, which team wins?

Extra Drill - Heading
Throw, Head, Catch

Drill - Suitable for Ages 5-10

Created Using www.SoccerTutor.com Tactics Manager Software

Organization

A 40x30 yard square is set out using marker cones with two 10x30 yard end zones also clearly marked. The players are split into two teams. All the players spread themselves out within the middle zone of the pitch. The ball can only be passed onto a team mate by following the simple rule, throw, head and catch.

Description

The game begins with the first player throwing the ball to the second player who has to head it onto the third player who catches it before throwing it on again. The two teams compete to score by heading the ball to one of their team mates so they can catch it in the end zone. The teams can only win possession of the ball by intercepting a header and catching the ball before the other player.

Coaching Points to Improve Heading in this drill.

1. Approach – The players should always watch the ball.
2. Body Shape - The players should have their eyes open and mouths closed. They have their mouths shut so they don't shut it on their tongues when they head the ball.
3. Contact – The forehead should contact through the centre of the underneath of the ball to head up and away (defensive header) or through the centre of the top of the ball to head down (attacking header).
4. End Product - The header is directed toward a team mate who can catch the ball.

Progressions and Drill Variations

For Younger Players.

1. Less players, make the game a 4v4 small sided game.

For Older or Better Players.

1. Use small target goals instead of an end zone.
2. Use goals with goalkeepers, to score the players have to head the ball past the goalkeeper and into the goal.

Fun

Keep the score, which team wins?

Extra Drill - Heading Triangles

Drill - Suitable for Ages 5-8

Created Using www.SoccerTutor.com Tactics Manager Software

Organization

Set out three goals using marker cones or traffic cones a suitable distance apart for the strength and age of the players. Three players are then positioned, one in each goal and one ball is used.

Description

The game begins with the first player throwing the ball to the second player. The second player then heads the ball at the third players goal trying to score. The third player having the ball now throws it to the first player, who heads it at the second players goal. The second player then gets the ball and throws it to the third player, who heads it at the first players goal. The drill can then continue with all the players getting the chance to head at goal.

Coaching Points to Improve Heading in this drill.

1. Approach – The players should be steady and always watching the ball.
2. Body Shape - The players should have their eyes open and mouths closed, so they don't shut their mouths on their tongues when they head the ball.
3. Contact – The forehead should contact through the centre of the top of the ball to head down into the goal.
4. End Product - The header is directed downward past the player and into the goal.

Progressions and Drill Variations

For Younger Players.

1. Make the area smaller and the goals bigger.

For Older or Better Players.

1. Use smaller target goals.
2. Encourage the players to play as goalkeepers and try to save the header.

Fun

Keep the score, which player is the most accurate scoring the most goals?

Extra Drill - Turns
Half Turn Drill

Drill - Suitable for Ages 7-10

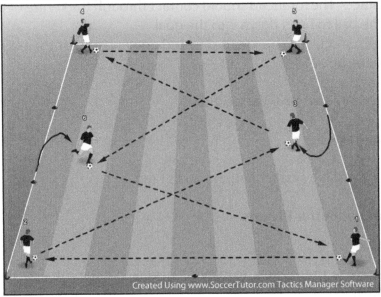

Organization

Set out a rectangle 30x20 using marker cones. Six players take up positions on the cones, one on each corner cone and then the two other players on the middle cones as shown.

Description

The drill begins with the first player passing the ball across the base line from right to left. The second player lets the ball come across their body and receives the ball with their left foot. The second player then plays the ball diagonally forward to the third player who runs toward the ball before letting the ball come across their body receiving it on the right foot, in front of them and facing forward (half turned). The ball is then passed diagonally forward to player four who passes across to player five. They let the ball come across them to receive on the left foot before passing to six who moves toward the ball receiving it half turned in front of them ready to pass it back to player one for the drill to start again.

Coaching Points to Improve Turning in this drill.

1. Approach – The players should be on their toes, watching the ball and waiting for the pass.
2. Body Shape - The players should be alert, steady and comfortable.
3. Contact – The player lets the ball come across the front of their body to receive the ball facing forward and therefore able to see all around them and easily pass the ball forward. The player should trap the ball with the inside of the furthest foot from the player passing the ball. If the ball was played across from the right they should trap with the inside of the left foot. The ball should be trapped within the players control area.
4. End Product - The pass to the next player needs to be well weighted and accurate.

Progressions and Drill Variations

For Younger Players.

1. Make the area smaller.
2. Swap the players around to make sure they all get the chance to play in all the positions, corners and middle cones.

For Older or Better Players.

1. Add a defender at both of the middle cones to promote the movement of the receiving player. They need to sprint away from the defender and come to receive the ball in space in order to receive it half turned.

Fun

How many correct turns and passes can be made before an error is made, can they beat the last score?

Extra Drill - Turns
Turn to Shoot

Drill - Suitable for Ages 7-10

Created Using www.SoccerTutor.com Tactics Manager Software

Organization

Set out a 30x30 square using marker cones. A goal is placed at the centre of one of the sides and a goalkeeper is added. Three players (servers) are positioned along the top of the square and each given a number 1,2 and 3. Four players are then placed in the square and play 2v2 in the square. One of the pairs are the attackers and the other pair are the defenders.

Description

The drill begins with the coach shouting a number 1,2 or 3 the server matching this number then plays the ball into the best placed attacker. The attacking player needs to receive the ball, turn and shoot at goal. The two players in the square can also interchange passes if needed but they should be encouraged to try and turn or receive the ball half turned in order to get a shot off as soon as possible. After a set number of attempts the attackers and defenders should change roles. Remember to swap the servers so they get a chance to participate as defenders and attackers.

Coaching Points to Improve Turning in this drill.

1. Approach – The attacking players should be listening for the call, watching for the pass and the defenders around them.
2. Body Shape - The players should be steady and comfortable.
3. Contact – The attacker should try and get away from the defender to receive the ball half tuned. If they cannot get away they need to receive the ball with a long barrier and turn away from the defender.
4. Technique - Was the half turn or turn performed correctly.
5. End Product - The shot should be on target.

Progressions and Drill Variations

For Younger Players.

1. Make the area larger.
2. Make the defenders passive.

For Older or Better Players.

1. Make the area smaller.
2. Make sure the defenders press and all the players work at full speed.

Fun

How many goals can each of the teams score during their turn as attackers?

Give the defenders a goal if they can challenge and win the ball off the attackers.

Extra Drill - Dribbling
Take on the Defenders

Drill - Suitable for Ages 5-8

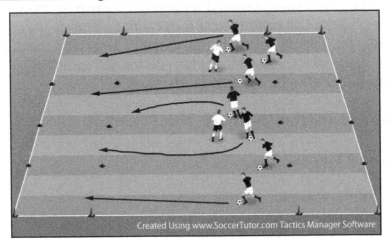

Created Using www.SoccerTutor.com Tactics Manager Software

Organization

A 40x30 yard square is set out using marker cones with two 10 yard end zones also clearly marked. Two players are given the role of defenders with everyone else attacking. Each attacker gets a ball and stands in one of the end zones, the two defenders stand in the central area.

Description

On the coaches command the attackers dribble forward and attempt to dribble their ball past the defenders and into the opposite end zone. The defenders try to tackle the attackers and kick their balls out of the playing area. Any attacker who loses their ball is eliminated from the game. The attackers, on the coaches command, keep dribbling from one end zone to the other until they are all eliminated.

Coaching Points to Improve Dribbling in this drill.

1. Attitude - Be positive at all times the player should always believe they will get past the defenders into the end zone.
2. Approach - The approach should be controlled and thoughtful. The player should not look down at the ball but ahead of it so they can see both the ball and the defender coming to meet them.
3. Decision - The player needs to make a clear decision early, where are they going and how will they get past the defender. Which trick or move will they use.
4. Contact - The contact depends on where the player wants to go.
5. Exploit the space - After getting past the defender the player should accelerate away and leave the defender unable to recover as they race into the end zone.

Progressions and Drill Variations

For Younger Players.

1. Make the area bigger or only have one defender.

For Older or Better Players.

1. Make the width of the square thinner keeping the length or extending it.
2. Whenever a player is eliminated they become a defender.

Fun

The last two players left as attackers become the defenders for the next game. Who can win? Who will be the last one standing?

Extra Drill - Dribbling
Dribbling Diagonal Goals

Small Sided Game - Suitable for Ages 7-10

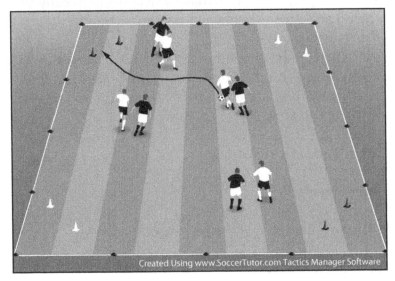

Created Using www.SoccerTutor.com Tactics Manager Software

Organization

A 30x30 yard square is set out using marker cones. Four goals are set out using traffic cones and these are placed one in each corner. The four goals should be in two colours and the same coloured goals should be placed diagonally opposite, as shown. The players are split into two teams of four.

Description

The two teams attack and defend the two opposite coloured goals. For example the white shirted players are attacking the two dark goals and defending the two light goals whilst the dark shirted team attack the light goals and defend the dark goals. The drill starts with the coach rolling the ball into the area. Both teams challenge for possession of the ball and try to dribble the ball through one of the two goals they are attacking to score a goal.

Coaching Points to Improve Dribbling in this drill.

1. Attitude - Be positive at all times the player should always believe they will dribble through the goals.
2. Approach - The approach should be controlled and thoughtful. The player should not look down at the ball but ahead of it so they can see both the ball and any defenders around them.
3. Decision - The player needs to make a clear decision early, which goal are they attacking and how will they get past any defender who might be in the way. They should also think about the decision to dribble or pass.
4. Technique - The quality of the player dribbling or passing the ball.
5. Exploit the space - After getting past the defender the player should accelerate away and leave the defender unable to recover as they race toward the goal.

Progressions and Drill Variations

For Younger Players.

1. Make the area bigger.
2. Make the goals bigger.
3. Add a neutral player to play with the team in possession.

For Older or Better Players.

1. Make the square smaller.
2. Give the teams a time limit.

Fun

Keep the score and award bonus goals for taking players on or a new trick to get around a defender.

Which team is the first to score five goals?

Extra Drill - Goalkeeping
Shoot, Save. Shoot, Save

Drill - Suitable for Ages 6-10

Created Using www.SoccerTutor.com Tactics Manager Software

Organization

A 20x20 yard square or the penally area of a standard pitch can be used for this drill. One goalkeeper is used in a standard mini-soccer goal. Two sets of traffics cones are set out, two marking a distance 12 yards from the goal and another two marking 18 yards from the goal. Five players are positioned in a line beyond the furthest cones and five balls are placed roughly 5 yards from the goal.

Description

On the coaches command the goalkeeper begins the drill by running to the first ball and side foot passing it toward the first player. As soon as the ball gets past the first set of cones (12 yards out) the player can run forward and shoot at goal. The goalkeeper should take a couple of steps backwards after passing the ball and then set themselves ready to react and save. The goalkeeper then moves forward to pass the second ball to the second player. The goalkeeper attempts to save again and the drill continues passing to the third, fourth and fifth players.

Coaching Points to Improve Goalkeeping in this drill.

1. Approach – The goalkeeper should take a couple of steps to move in line with the ball. They should always watch the ball. The goalkeeper has to get into their set position ready to make the save as soon as the players foot is ready to strike the ball.
2. Body Shape - The goalkeepers "set position" The goalkeeper should have their feet placed shoulder width apart and be leaning slightly forward waiting to receive the ball.
3. Contact – The players should scoop the ball up into their arms when the shot is hit along the floor. They should "Cup" the ball when the shot is at waist height. Any higher and the goalkeeper should use the "W" where their hands and fingers are splayed upwards and outwards with the thumbs almost touching.

Progressions and Drill Variations

For Younger Players.

1. Make the distance smaller.
2. Have three strikers.

For Older or Better Players.

1. Make the first cone distance greater, further to shoot from.
2. Allow the striker to shoot earlier, narrow the distance between the two cones.

Fun

Give everyone the chance to go in goal and keep the scores of each individual. Which player can save the most shots?

Watch out for the spectacular saves, cheer them on and promote success.

Extra Drill - Goalkeeping
Dive, Up, Dive, Up, Dive, Up

Drill - Suitable for Ages 7-10

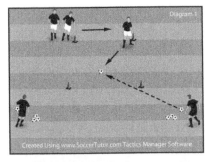
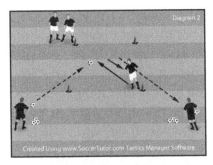
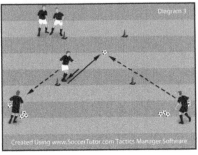
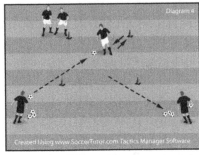

Organization

A 7x7 yard square is marked out using traffic cones. The players line up waiting to start at the furthest cone on the left hand side. Two coaches (servers) with balls are positioned diagonally out from the front two cones about 5 yards.

Description

On the coaches command the goalkeeper moves across the back of the square to touch the top of the back right cone. The coach bottom right throws the ball toward the centre of the square (diagram 1). The goalkeeper facing the coach dives to their left to save and throw the ball back. The goalkeeper follows the throw to touch the cone front right then turns to face the coach front left. The coach throws the ball and the goalkeeper dives right to save (diagram 2) The goalkeeper throws the ball back and again the goalkeeper follows the ball to touch the front left cone and then dives back to the left to save a throw from the front right coach (diagram 3). They throw the ball back again and run back to touch the back right cone before coming forward to save a throw from the front left coach (diagram 4).

Coaching Points to Improve Goalkeeping in this drill.

1. Approach – The goalkeeper should be rapid through the drill but take small side steps to move diagonally across the square while facing and watching the ball, waiting for the throws.
2. Body Shape - The goalkeeper moves using small steps, maximum shoulder width apart in order to get into the set position as early as possible after the ball is thrown.
3. Contact – The players should dive diagonally forward using the "W" technique where their hands and fingers are splayed outwards with the thumbs almost touching. The goalkeeper should lead with both hands to save, imagine them to be almost handcuffed together.

Progressions and Drill Variations

For Younger Players.

1. Make the cone distances smaller.
2. Make the throws easy paced and slightly to the sides.

For Older or Better Players.

1. Throw the ball quicker, as soon as the goalkeeper touches the cones to raise the tempo of the drill.
2. Throw the ball wider to extend the goalkeepers dive.
3. Promote the need to speed up the recovery from the save and continue the drill.
4. If they cope with the throws in the previous drill try it faster and further for their next attempt.

Fun

How fast can they go and how far can they dive to catch the ball.

Extra Drill - Long Lofted Passing
Lofted Pass Target Goals

Drill - Suitable for Ages 5-8

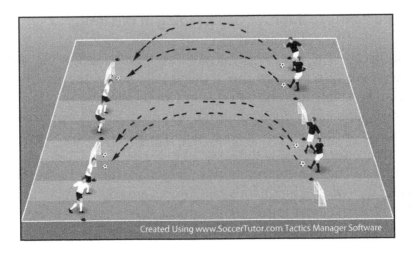

Created Using www.SoccerTutor.com Tactics Manager Software

Organization

Two sets of marker cones are placed 20 yards apart. Two target goals are placed on each side (not opposite but offset) The players are split into two teams and stand on each side opposite the target goals.

Description

The players from one team on one side of the area are given a ball each, in this case the dark shirted players on the right. On the coaches command the players on one side try a long lofted pass into the target goals on the opposite side. The players should try to loft the ball directly into the goal, without bouncing. The balls are collected by the team opposite and then, again on the coaches command, they take their turn to loft a pass into the target goals.

Coaching Points to Improve Long Lofted Passing in this drill.

1. Approach - The player approaches the ball slightly from the side.
2. Body shape - The standing foot should be slightly back from the side of the ball resulting in the kicking foot slightly reaching for the ball.
3. Contact - The top of the foot, a little above the base of the big toe, contacts with the underside of the middle of the ball.
4. Follow through - A big and high follow through with the kicking foot to gain height and power.

Progressions and Drill Variations

For Younger Players.

1. Make the area thinner.
2. Allow the players to score in the target goal with one bounce.
3. Make the goals bigger.

For Older or Better Players.

1. Make the area wider.
2. Make the goals smaller.
3. Use target cones, Can the players hit those without the ball bouncing.

Fun

Which team scores the most goals? Keep the scores and keep the competition going.

Extra Drill - Long Lofted Passing
Long Lofted Pass and Move

Drill - Suitable for Ages 7-10

Created Using www.SoccerTutor.com Tactics Manager Software

Organization

A 20x20 yard square is set out using marker cones with target cones in the corners. The players are split with half standing at one corner and the others at the other corner diagonally opposite. A player from each line of players in the corner stands about 5 yards in along one of the sides. Shown above players (1)and (4)

Description

The drill starts at one corner with the first player (2) in the line. This player passes the ball to the player on the edge (1) who plays the ball back to them (one-two) before running around the area and joining the line opposite. The player (2) continues by playing a lofted pass across the square to the first player in the line at the opposite corner (3) This player (2) then takes the place of the player on the edge (1) The player receiving the ball (3) plays a one two with the player on the side of the area near them (4). The drill continues with another cross field lofted pass by them (3) back to the opposite line again. They (3) take the place of the player on the edge (4) and this player (4) runs round to join the opposite line.

Coaching Points to Improve Long Lofted Passing in this drill.

1. Approach - The player approaches the ball slightly from the side.
2. Body shape - The standing foot should be slightly back from the side of the ball resulting in the kicking foot slightly reaching for the ball.
3. Contact - The top of the foot, a little above the base of the big toe, contacts with the underside of the middle of the ball.
4. Follow through - A big and high follow through with the kicking foot to gain height and power.

Progressions and Drill Variations

For Younger Players.

1. Make the area smaller.

For Older or Better Players.

1. Make the area larger.
2. Make the players sprint around the square to join the other line.
3. Promote receiving skills, can they use their chest, knee or head to control the ball before laying the ball off with their second touch.
4. Can they receive and lay off in one touch.

Fun

Can they play an accurate long lofted pass that goes directly to the player so they don't need to move to collect the ball? Award points for passing quality and control.

Preparation Drill - Teams First Formation Drill
Simple Halves Game

Drill - Suitable for Ages 5-6

Created Using www.SocerTutor.com Tactics Manager Software

Organization

A 60x40 yard pitch is marked out with four traffic cones in the corners and marker cones all around. You may need to change the size of the pitch to make it more suitable to the size and power of your players. Place marker cones across the centre of the pitch as a half way line. The players are split into two teams and each team has half its players in the attacking half and half in the defensive half.

Description

The game is played as normal but with one simple rule. All the players have to stay in their half of the pitch. The only way the ball can get from one half to the other is through a pass. Swap the players half way through the game. The defenders become attackers and vice-versa so each player gets a chance to play as a defender or attacker.

Variation - Easier Still.

Give the defenders an overload in their half (3v2, 4v3) to help them gain possession and promote passing forward.

Team Formation End Game - Teams First Wing Drill
Simple Wing Drill

Drill - Suitable for Ages 6-8 or for setting up a new team

This drill is included for use with a new team embarking on a season of Mini-Soccer where the actual understanding of team shape and roles is required. It should in all cases be used alongside small sided games, technical games and drills where player development is paramount.

Organization

Created Using www.SoccerTutor.com Tactics Manager Software

A 30x30 yard pitch is marked out with four traffic cones in the corners and marker cones all around. A goal is placed at the centre of the far side of the square. Marker cones are placed 5 yards in at each side to form wing channels. The players play in your teams formation attacking a goal. In our drill we have one serving midfield player, two wide players, an advanced midfielder and striker. A goalkeeper is in the goal ahead.

Description

The server starts the drill by passing the ball forward to one of the wide midfielders. As in a game they take the ball forward and deliver the cross for the players to try and score. The drill can then be repeated with the server passing their ball to the opposite wide player.

Coaching Points to Improve Team Shape / Understanding

1. Server - The deep midfield player needs to play the ball in front of the winger so they can receive the ball going toward goal. They should then move forward to support but only 10 yards or so
2. Winger - Can they be positive and take a good first touch to move forward. Can they get a cross over into the attackers? The winger who does not receive the ball should start to move forward and infield to support the attack around the back post.
3. Attacking Midfielder - Can they move forward to support the attack and any ball crossed behind the striker.
4. Striker - The striker should turn out from the winger with the ball and then turn inward to attack the ball and near post.
5. End Product - Always be upbeat with younger players. Praise crosses and shots on target.

Progressions and Drill Variations

For Younger Players.

1. Remove the goalkeeper.
2. Make the area smaller.

For Older or Better Players.

1. Bring in a central defender.

Team Formation End Game - Teams First Formation Drill
Coaching Simple Team Structure

Drill - Suitable for Ages 6-8 or for setting up a new team

This drill is included for use with a new team embarking on a season of Mini-Soccer where team shape and tactics is required. It should in all cases be used alongside small sided games, technical games and drills where player development is paramount.

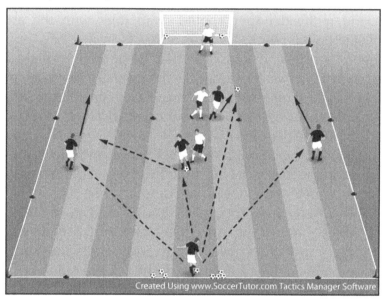

Created Using www.SoccerTutor.com Tactics Manager Software

Organization

A 30x30 yard pitch is marked out with four traffic cones in the corners and marker cones all around. A goal is placed at the centre of the far side of the square. Marker cones are placed 10 yards from the goal line to form an attacking end zone. The players play in your teams formation attacking a goal. In our drill we have one serving midfield player, two wide players, an advanced midfielder and striker. A goalkeeper is in the goal ahead.

Description

The server starts the drill by passing the ball forward to any of the players, as shown. The game is then live and players react as in a game trying to attack the goal while the defenders try to win back possession. When the ball goes out of play the drill is restarted by the server. Rotate the players so they all get an understanding of the positions.

Coaching Points to Improve Team Shape / Understanding

1. Server - The deep midfield player needs to watch to see which players create space for the pass before playing the ball into them. They should then move forward to support. If they go beyond the attacking midfielder they should swap roles with the attacking midfielder holding back.
2. Winger - On receiving a pass can they be positive and take a good first touch to move forward. Can they get a cross over into the attackers? The winger who does not receive the ball should start to move forward and infield to support the attack around the back post.
3. Attacking Midfielder - Can they receive and play the ball out to a wide player, bounce the ball with the server or turn and play in the striker.
4. Striker - Can the striker get free from the defender to receive the ball between them and the goal to run onto or come short to receive. If it goes to a wide player the striker should turn out from the winger with the ball and then turn inward to attack the ball and near post.
5. Defenders - Can they get goal side of the player being marked but also ball side. Ball side means they are on the shoulder of the opponent nearer the ball so the can always see it and also possibly nip in and nick any ball passed into the player they are marking.

Progressions and Drill Variations

For Younger Players.

1. Remove the goalkeeper.
2. Remove defenders and place traffic cones.

For Older or Better Players.

1. Bring in more defenders.

Final Words

We hope this book helps you in your coaching and more importantly helps you help your young players improve. Good luck with your teams.

If you want more tips and drills visit us at www.SoccerTutor.com.

More great Coaching Books from

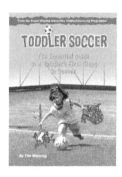

To order Books, DVDs, Software, Magazines, Equipment or Teamwear;

Visit: www.SoccerTutor.com
Call UK:+44 208 1234 007 | US: 305-767-4443

Lightning Source UK Ltd.
Milton Keynes UK
UKOW06f1232131113

221014UK00006B/315/P